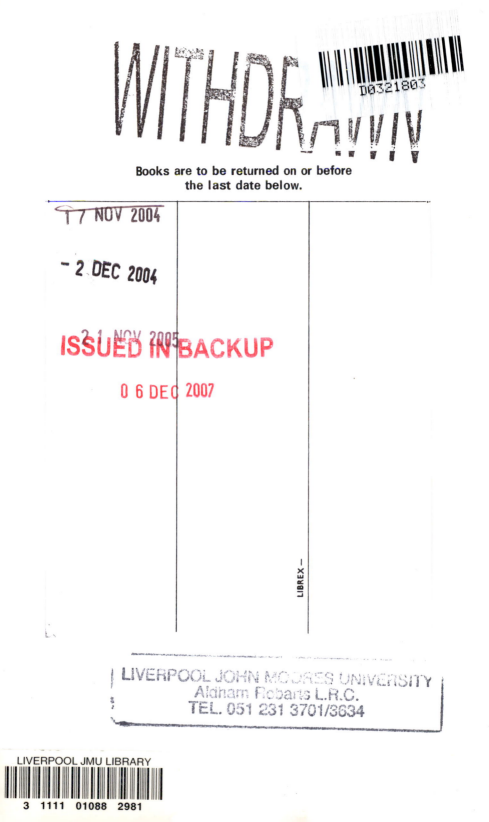

WITHDRAWN

Books are to be returned on or before
the last date below.

Translation/History/Culture

Translation Studies
General editors: Susan Bassnett and André Lefevere

In the same series:

Translation, Rewriting, and the Manipulation of Literary Fame
André Lefevere

Translation, Poetics and the Stage
Six French *Hamlets*
Romy Heylen

Translation/History/Culture

A Sourcebook

Edited by André Lefevere

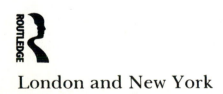

London and New York

First published 1992
by Routledge
11 New Fetter Lane, London EC4P 4EE

Simultaneously published in the USA and Canada
by Routledge
a division of Routledge, Chapman and Hall, Inc.
29 West 35th Street, New York, NY 10001

Transferred to digital printing 2002

Routledge is an imprint of the Taylor & Francis Group

Typeset in 10 on 12 point Baskerville
by Computerset, Harmondsworth, Middlesex
Printed in Great Britain by Intype London Ltd

British Library Cataloguing in Publication Data
A catalogue record for this book is available from the
British Library.

Library of Congress Cataloging in Publication Data
  Translation/History/Culture: a sourcebook / [translated
and edited by] André Lefevere.
    p.   cm.
  A collection of texts in English with commentary of
writings about translation originally written in English,
French, German, and Latin between the birth of Cicero
in 106 BC and the death in 1931 of Ulrich von
Willamowitz-Mollendorff.
  Includes bibliographical references and index.
  1. Translating and interpreting –
History. 2. Language and culture.   I. Lefevere,
André.
  P306.T735   1992
  418'.02—dc20   92-6010

ISBN 0-415-07697-8
    0-415-07698-6 (pbk)

Two things can be held against me in connection with this translation: one concerns the selection of the work, the other the way in which I have translated it. One group of people will say that I should not have translated this particular author, another group that I should not have translated him in this way.

Nicolas Perrot d'Ablancourt

Contents

General editors' preface

The growth of Translation Studies as a separate discipline is a success story of the 1980s. The subject has developed in many parts of the world and is clearly destined to continue developing well into the 21st century. Translation studies brings together work in a wide variety of fields, including linguistics, literary study, history, anthropology, psychology and economics. This series of books will reflect the breadth of work in Translation Studies and will enable readers to share in the exciting new developments that are taking place at the present time.

Translation is, of course, a rewriting of an original text. All rewritings, whatever their intention, reflect a certain ideology and a poetics and as such manipulate literature to function in a given society in a given way. Rewriting is manipulation, undertaken in the service of power, and in its positive aspect can help in the evolution of a literature and a society. Rewritings can introduce new concepts, new genres, new devices, and the history of translation is the history also of literary innovation, of the shaping power of one culture upon another. But rewriting can also repress innovation, distort and contain, and in an age of ever increasing manipulation of all kinds, the study of the manipulative processes of literature as exemplified by translation can help us towards a greater awareness of the world in which we live.

Since this series of books on Translation Studies is the first of its kind, it will be concerned with its own genealogy. It will publish texts from the past that illustrate its concerns in the present, and will publish texts of a more theoretical nature immediately addressing those concerns, along with case studies illustrating manipulation through rewriting in various literatures. It will be comparative in nature and will range through many literary traditions both Western and non-Western. Through the concepts of rewriting and manipulation, this series aims to tackle the problem of ideology, change and power in literature and society and so assert the central function of translation as a shaping force.

Susan Bassnett
André Lefevere

Preface

This collection contains what many consider to be some of the most important, or at least most seminal texts produced over centuries of thinking about translation in Western Europe in Latin, French, German, and English. The collection spans approximately the twenty centuries that elapsed between the birth, in 106 BC, of the Roman orator, statesman, and translator Marcus Tullius Cicero and the death, in 1931 AD, of the German classical scholar and translator Ulrich von Willamowitz-Moellendorff. No attempt has been made to include modern or contemporary texts. These should, and will, be gathered in other collections to be published in the series for which the present collection endeavors to establish a modest genealogy.

A fair number of the texts collected here have been much referred to, infrequently quoted, and even more rarely read since they have not all previously been available in English. I have translated anew all the texts printed here, except for those originally written in English, and I have tried to select texts that should provide the essential background for current thinking about the translation of literature.

Not all texts collected here have by any means been translated or printed in their entirety. To do so would have necessitated the production of a book several times the size of this one. Moreover, a fair number of well-known texts on translation tend, on closer inspection, to say relatively little about translation while touching on a wide variety of other topics. I have, accordingly, limited myself to those extracts which bear directly on translation, as in Luther's famous *Letter*, for example, where I have excluded the (great majority of) passages dealing with all kinds of disputes between the German rulers of his time.

The texts have been arranged thematically, rather than chronologically. It is my conviction that translations are made under a
number of constraints of which language is arguably the least
important. I have therefore arranged the shorter texts according to
the constraint they seem to address most obviously. Some texts deal
with ideological constraints on the production of translations, with
the power of patronage to enforce these constraints, with constraints
of a more poetical nature, with so-called Universe of Discourse
constraints and, finally, with both constraints imposed by the structure of different languages and attempts to expand the scope of
languages in spite of these constraints. Other texts raise the
question of the position of a central text in a culture and of a central
culture in a configuration of cultures. Still other texts deal with the
role translation has traditionally played in education. A final
category of texts deals mainly with the technique of actual translating, usually in the form of lists of rules.

It is hoped that this arrangement will highlight the important
topics that should be covered in any discussion of literary translation
more effectively than any chronological arrangement could have
done, even though the texts have been arranged chronologically
within their respective sections, for reasons of historical continuity.
Needless to say, I found myself pleasantly surprised and more than
a little envious to discover the constraints I thought I had identified
and elevated to the status of organizational categories neatly set out
in Madame Dacier's introduction to her translation of the *Iliad*. This
illuminating text therefore occupies the position of a "second introduction" to the present collection.

Both my surprise and my envy are symptomatic of current
thinking on literary translation. Much of what we are saying has
been said already, albeit in a different kind of jargon. This should
not deter us, however. Looking back at the long tradition of
thinking on translation in Western Europe, we realize that relatively
recent attempts to limit discussions of translation to what pertains to
constraints of language only, signally fail to do justice to the complexity of the problem. Furthermore, knowledge of the tradition,
the genealogy of our thinking, helps us to focus not just on problems
concerning translation as such, but also on ways in which the study
of translation can be made productive for cultural studies in general.
We are finally beginning to realize that translation deserves to
occupy a much more central position in cultural history than the one
to which it is currently relegated.

Acknowledgments

I would like to express my deep gratitude and great appreciation to Mr Roger Tavernier, chief bibliographer of the University Library in Leuven, Flanders, without whose help I would not have been able to gain access to some of the texts translated here, and most especially to my colleague and friend Dr Judith Woodsworth of Concordia University, Montreal, who has worked miracles proofreading the manuscript.

Introduction

A translation, says Petrus Danielus Huetius in a text translated in this collection, is "a text written in a well-known language which refers to and represents a text in a language which is not as well known." This, to my mind, is the most productive definition of a translation made within the tradition represented here, simply because it raises many, if not all of the relevant questions at once.

First of all, why is it necessary to represent a foreign text in one's own culture? Does the very fact of doing that not amount to an admission of the inadequacy of that culture? Secondly, who makes the text in one's own culture "represent" the text in the foreign culture? In other words: who translates, why, and with what aim in mind? Who selects texts as candidates to "be represented?" Do translators? And are those translators alone? Are there other factors involved? Thirdly, how do members of the receptor culture know that the imported text is well represented? Can they trust the translator(s)? If not, who can they trust, and what can they do about the whole situation, short of not translating at all? If a translation is, indeed, a text that represents another, the translation will to all intents and purposes function as that text in the receptor culture, certainly for those members of that culture who do not know the language in which the text was originally written. Let us not forget that translations are made by people who do not need them for people who cannot read the originals. Fourthly, not all languages seem to have been created equal. Some languages enjoy a more prestigious status than others, just as some texts occupy a more central position in a given culture than others – the Bible, for instance, or the qur'an. Fifthly, why produce texts that "refer to" other texts? Why not simply produce originals in the first place?

So much for the questions. Now for some tentative answers, culled from the genealogy drawn up in this collection. If you produce a text that "refers to" another text, rather than producing your own, you are most likely to do so because you think the other text enjoys a prestige far greater than the prestige your own text might possibly aspire to. In other words, you invoke the authority of the text you represent. It may be a sobering thought that some of the masterpieces of world literature, such as Cervantes' *Don Quixote*, profess to be translations of lost originals, i.e. that they refer to non-existent texts in order to derive some kind of legitimacy which, it is felt, would otherwise not be present to the same extent.

Translation has to do with authority and legitimacy and, ultimately, with power, which is precisely why it has been and continues to be the subject of so many acrimonious debates. Translation is not just a "window opened on another world," or some such pious platitude. Rather, translation is a channel opened, often not without a certain reluctance, through which foreign influences can penetrate the native culture, challenge it, and even contribute to subverting it. "When you offer a translation to a nation," says Victor Hugo, "that nation will almost always look on the translation as an act of violence against itself."

No wonder nations have always felt they needed some person or persons they could trust enough to entrust him or her with the task of translating: the Horatian "fidus interpres," or "trustworthy interpreter." It is important to remember that the trust is invested in the producer of the translation, not necessarily in the product itself. "Trusted" translators, like the group of translators who produced the Septuagint, in fact produced what is generally acknowledged as a relatively "bad" translation, but one that continues to function to this day as the "official" translation used by the Greek Orthodox Church. Trust may be more important than quality. Translations which members of a culture have come to trust may mean more to them than translations that can claim to represent the original better. Witness the following extract from one of St Augustine's letters to St Jerome:

> When one of our brothers, a bishop, had introduced the use of your translation in the church of which he is the pastor, the congregation hit upon a passage in the prophet Jonah which you translated in a very different way from the way in which it had established itself in the mind and memory of all, and the

way it has been sung for such a long time. Great unrest arose among the people, especially since the Greeks protested and began to shout about falsification in a vituperative manner. As a result the bishop – it happened in the town of Onea – saw himself forced to rely on the Jews who lived in the city to clear up the matter. But they replied, either out of ignorance or out of malice, that the Hebrew manuscripts contained exactly what was also to be found in the Greek and Latin manuscripts. And then what? To escape from great danger the man was forced to correct himself, as if he had made a mistake, since he did not want to lose all the people in his church.

Obviously, trust is most important where the most central text of a culture is concerned, a text invoked to legitimize the power of those who wield it in that culture. It may just be possible that the West has paid so much attention to translation because its central text, the Bible, was written in a language it could not readily understand, so that it was forced to rely on translators to legitimize power. The other alternative was, of course, not to translate the central text at all, but to have those whose lives are ruled by it learn the language it is written in, or at least go through the necessary motions in that direction, as in the case of the Qur'an.

Huetius puts the matter in similar terms when he quotes St Jerome as saying

One word should be translated by one word in Holy Writ, *where even the order of the words is a mystery*, where a construction that has not been refined with great art often carries more than one sentence. Since the greater part of Holy Writ should not be studied for its elegance, however, Saint Jerome also admits that other texts should be translated in a different manner, nor does he always follow his own precepts.

Trust is one thing, expertise another. Not only does Huetius point to the ever present gulf between theory and practice, between what translators profess to be doing and what they actually do, he also suggests that trust need not be absolute in all cases. Translators can be trusted more with texts that are not central to the culture as a whole since they can only do limited damage at worst. Or, to put it simply in text–linguistic terms: different types of texts need to be translated in different ways.

The same reasoning has also been extended to different cultures. Whereas translators in the West have held Greek and Latin works in high esteem, as representing the expression of prestigious cultures within the Western world view, they have treated other cultures, not thought to enjoy a similar prestige, in a very different manner indeed. Edward Fitzgerald, translator of the *Rubaiyat* of Omar Khayyam, for instance, wrote to his friend E. B. Cowell in 1857: "It is an amusement for me to take what Liberties I like with these Persians, who (as I think) are not Poets enough to frighten one from such excursions, and who really do want a little Art to shape them." The "little Art" represents a liberal dose of Western poetics (the accepted concept of what a poem should be) and Western Universe of Discourse (legs of lamb, not felt to be sufficiently poetic, are left out of the translation of the *Rubaiyat*), but not Western ideology, since the point of the translation is also to demonstrate that other societies have been able to live with an ideology radically different from the one dominant in Fitzgerald's time.

Yet there is one situation in which the West has traditionally allowed liberties to be taken with Latin and Greek texts: that of language learning, either by the individual or by a whole nation. The "locus classicus" is probably the following statement by Cicero:

> I decided to take speeches written in Greek by great orators and to translate them freely, and I obtained the following results: by giving a Latin form to the text I had read I could not only make use of the best expressions in common usage with us, but I could also coin new expressions, analogous to those used in Greek, and they were no less well received by our people as long as they seemed appropriate.

Translators are allowed more liberties on what one might be tempted to call "the purely linguistic level," certainly if the translation is not meant to "represent" the original in the translators' culture, but simply to help translators refine their knowledge of their own language. If translators do try to represent a text that claims to represent the original in their culture, liberties on the purely linguistic level will be tolerated when they are seen as potentially refining, improving, extending the language of the receiving culture. In this case readers can judge for themselves since they are no longer judging the correspondence of original and translation but rather the wording of the translation which is, after all, written in their own language.

But what if language is not primarily considered an ornament, something belonging more or less squarely in the realm of rhetoric, as it was in the Renaissance? If one maintains with Schleiermacher that "every man is in the power of the language he speaks and all his thinking is a product thereof," it is no longer possible to separate the "substance" of a text from its "ornaments" and to re-express that substance by means of different ornaments. Contrary to what Batteux affirms, the translator will no longer be "forgiven all metaphors as long as he makes sure the thought keeps the same body and the same life." If in Schleiermacher's pre-Wittgensteinian and pre-deconstructionist belief thought is always inscribed and, to a great extent, prescribed by language, translation nears the edge of the impossible. Since no (wo)man can leave his or her own "language game" the mere attempt to do so is a crime.

Schleiermacher goes on to say that "it is an act that runs counter to both nature and morality to become a deserter to one's own mother tongue and to give oneself to another." Here lies the origin of the concept that translators should translate only into their mother tongues, and that translators are responsible for the integrity of both the cultures to which they belong and the texts they translate. Rather than leaving "the reader in peace as much as possible," and "moving the author towards him," thus naturalizing what is foreign, the translator should in Schleiermacher's opinion leave "the author in peace, as much as possible," and "move the reader towards him." A translation should therefore sound "foreign" enough to its reader for that reader to discern the workings of the original language that expresses the language game, the culture of which the original was a part, shining through the words on the translated page. Obviously this is a type of translation no longer practiced in our day and age, simply because the audience for it has almost ceased to exist. Schleiermacher and some of his contemporaries produced their translations not for the monolingual reader who has no access whatsoever to the original, but rather for the educated reader who was able to read original and translation side by side and, in doing so, to appreciate the difference in linguistic expression as expressing the difference between two language games.

Translation then, is not just a process that happens in the translator's head. Readers decide to accept or reject translations.

Different types of reader will require different types of translation. In Goethe's words: "if you want to influence the masses, a
simple translation is always best. Critical translations vying with
the original really are of use only for conversations the learned
conduct among themselves." Goethe was probably thinking of the
type of translation described in the previous paragraph when he
used the phrase "critical translations," but that phrase might just
as well be used for the type of translation of a work of literature
that is not produced with the intention of representing its original
as *literature* in the receiving culture. The literal, the interlinear,
and other such types of translation of literature are obviously not
aimed at influencing the masses, but rather at making the text of a
foreign work of literature accessible to scholarly analysis without
having it enter the body of literature in the receiving culture, even
though all scholarly translations do, to some extent, reflect the
poetics of the time in which they are written.

Yet much translation of literature wants to influence, if not the
masses, at least the literature of its own time in its own culture. To
do so, it wholeheartedly naturalizes the original. Most producers
of this type of translation will take Gaspard de Tende's advice: "if
you want to make a good translation, then you must not only make
everybody speak according to their habits and inclinations, but
you must also see to it that the way they express themselves is
rendered in simple and natural terms, which have already passed
into current usage." Once you begin to naturalize, however, you
realize that you cannot just stop at words. Rather, as Perrot
d'Ablancourt puts it in what is probably the first statement of the
much vaunted "principle" of "dynamic equivalence:"

> I do not always stick to the author's words, nor even to his
> thoughts. I keep the effect he wanted to produce in mind, and
> then I arrange the material after the fashion of our time.
> Different times do not just require different words, but also
> different thoughts, and ambassadors usually dress in the fash-
> ion of the country they are sent to, for fear of appearing
> ridiculous in the eyes of the people they try to please.

There are words and fashions (or objects or concepts, which
linguists tend to call the Universe of Discourse) but there is more.
Perrot d'Ablancourt says earlier in the same essay:

> I am the less to blame in that I have left out what was too filthy
> and softened what was too free, at least in some places. This is

how I justify my conduct, and the translation I attempted is justified by the many advantages that will come to the public from its reading of this author.

Not all features of the original are, it would seem, acceptable to the receiving culture, or rather to those who decide what is, or should be acceptable to that culture: the patrons who commission a translation, publish it, or see to it that it is distributed. The patron is the link between the translator's text and the audience the translator wants to reach. If translators do not stay within the perimeters of the acceptable as defined by the patron (an absolute monarch, for instance, but also a publisher's editor), the chances are that their translation will either not reach the audience they want it to reach or that it will, at best, reach that audience in a circuitous manner. Du Bellay was well aware of the power of patronage when he concluded his advice to translators with the almost never quoted: "What I say is not meant for those who, at the command of princes and great lords, translate the most famous Greek and Latin writers, since the obedience one owes to those persons admits of no excuse in these matters." Not very much later the Earl of Roscommon reflects a shift in patronage in his description of the (hack) translators of his own time: "I pity from my Soul unhappy Men/ Compelled by Want to prostitute their Pen,/ Who must, like Lawyers, either starve or plead,/ And follow, right or wrong, where Guineas lead." Perhaps the most eloquent "tribute" to the power of patronage comes from the pen of Martin Luther:

> We are aware of the scribbler in Dresden who stole my New Testament. He admitted that my German is good and sweet and he realized that he could not do better and yet he wanted to discredit it. So he took my New Testament as I wrote it, almost word for word, and he took my preface, my glosses, and my name away and wrote his name, his preface, and his glosses in their place. He is now selling my New Testament under his name. Oh, dear children, how hurt I was when his prince, in a terrible preface, forbade the reading of Luther's New Testament but ordered the scribbler's New Testament read, which is exactly the same as the one Luther wrote.

If nothing else, this statement should help lay to rest the persistent notion that translation is mainly a matter of dictionaries and grammars.

Patrons circumscribe the translators' ideological space; critics tend to circumscribe their poetological space. To make a foreign work of literature acceptable to the receiving culture, translators will often adapt it to the poetics of that receiving culture. De la Motte, for instance, justifies his cutting down of the *Iliad* to a work half the size of the original by remarking: "Would a theatre audience accept having characters come out during the intervals in a tragedy to tell us all that is going to happen next? Would it approve if the actions of the principal characters were interrupted by the business of the *confidants*? Certainly not." He was merely adapting the epic to the requirements of the genre that was dominant in his day and age: the tragedy. Any elements in the Homeric epic that went against the poetics of the tragedy quite simply had to be deleted for the translation to find any audience at all.

Two centuries later, Willamowitz-Moellendorff is less sanguine about a solution to the problems raised by a possible difference in poetics between the literature of the original and the receiving literature, but he is most certainly aware of it; witness the advice he gives to potential translators: "Whoever wants to try this should, in any case, look for a German form analogous to the original in mood and style; let him decide to what extent he can adapt himself to the form of the original. His intention as a translator will be a decisive factor and so will be his understanding of the text." The alternative has, of course, been for translators to introduce new forms into their native literatures based on forms they found in the literature to which their originals belonged. Whereas many formal innovations can be traced back to translators, rather than to writers in their own right, Goethe's "we should hope that literary history will plainly state who was the first to take this road in spite of so many obstacles" has, in many cases, remained little more than an empty statement.

When we speak of "a culture" or "the receiving culture," we would do well to remember that cultures are not monolithic entities, but that there is always a tension inside a culture between different groups, or individuals, who want to influence the evolution of that culture in the way they think best. Translations have been made with the intention of influencing the development of a culture. The statement by Luther quoted above makes this abundantly clear. Translations have been made with the intention of influencing the development of a literature, and this intention is reflected on the level of each of the four constraints under which translators operate. Perrot d'Ablancourt is talking about ideology when he states: "In fact, there are many passages I have translated word for word, at least to the extent to which that is possible in an elegant translation. There are also passages in which I have considered what ought to be said, or what I could say, rather than what he actually said." The Abbé Prévost is commenting on the Universe of Discourse in his translation of Richardson's *Pamela* when he remarks:

> I have suppressed English customs where they may appear shocking to other nations, or made them conform to customs prevalent in the rest of Europe. It seemed to me that those remainders of the old and uncouth British ways, which only habit prevents the British themselves from noticing, would dishonor a book in which manners should be noble and virtuous. To give the reader an accurate idea of my work, let me just say, in conclusion, that the seven volumes of the English edition, which would amount to fourteen volumes in my own, have been reduced to four.

D'Alembert has poetics in mind when he suggests that "we do not transfer the classics into our language to familiarize ourselves with their defects, but rather to enrich our literature with the best they have achieved. To translate them in extracts is not to mutilate them but rather to paint them in profile and to their advantage." Gaspard de Tende refers to genres or types of texts when he points out that "it would not be advisable to translate orations that need to be treated with some latitude into a precise style, very cut and dry, nor should you translate parables, which need to be short and precise, into a style that would allow them more latitude." And the Abbé Delille refers to register when he states: "I have always maintained that extreme faithfulness in translation results in extreme unfaithfulness. A word may be noble in Latin, and its French equivalent may be base."

Translators operate under the constraints listed above. They most definitely do not do so in a mechanistic universe in which they have no choice. Rather, they have the freedom to stay within the perimeters marked by the constraints, or to challenge those constraints by trying to move beyond them. Practicing translators are beginning to be aware of such constraints, and of the ways their predecessors have devised to deal with them. Scholars interested in the study of translation and cross-cultural communication are beginning to realize that the study of translation is much more than mere normative rule-giving designed to ensure the production of the "best" possible translations. In D'Alembert's words: "In all modes of writing, reason has given a small number of rules, whim has extended them, and from them pedantry has forged the irons prejudice respects and talent does not break." Translation is such a complex matter that it cannot be regulated in ways attempted in the eighteenth century, or later. Since it is such a complex matter it deserves better than the usual "spot the mistake" kind of criticism that all too often ends up on the level of personal attack. We would do well to remember Leonardo Bruni's words: "and can a man not be a good man and still be either completely ignorant of all that has pertains to writing, or not have the extensive experience I require of him? I don't call such a person a bad man, but merely a bad translator."

This collection is an attempt to influence the direction in which Translation Studies might most profitably develop. Translation needs to be studied in connection with power and patronage, ideology and poetics, with emphasis on the various attempts to shore up or undermine an existing ideology or an existing poetics. It also needs to be studied in connection with text-type and register, and in connection with attempts to integrate different Universes of Discourse. Translation Studies has begun to focus on attempts to make texts accessible and to manipulate them in the service of a certain poetics and/or ideology. Seen in this way translation can be studied as one of the strategies cultures develop to deal with what lies outside their boundaries and to maintain their own character while doing so – the kind of strategy that ultimately belongs in the realm of change and survival, not in dictionaries and grammars.

Anne Dacier, 1647–1720. French translator and philologist.

Extract from the introduction to her translation of the *Iliad*, published in 1699.

All the difficulties I have pondered can be reduced to five. The first derives both from the nature of things and from the nature of the poem in general, whose art is completely opposed to that false concept of art I referred to some time ago. How can anybody delude himself into thinking he will be able to give our century a taste for these austere poems? While they contain useful instruction hidden under a plot invented with great ingenuity, they fail to arouse our curiosity since we consider adventures to be touching and interesting only if they deal with love.

The second difficulty derives from the allegories and the fables these poems of Homer's are filled with. In most cases these allegories merely show us their exterior, which we do not have the power to pierce. In so doing they prevent us from feeling the beauty of that great poem and they even lead us to misjudge its spirit.

The third difficulty derives from the customs and the features characteristic of those heroic times, which appear too uncouth for our century, and at times even contemptible. We witness Achilles, Patroclos, Agamemnon, and Ulysses performing acts we call servile. How can they be well received in our time by people who are accustomed to the heroes of our romances, so well-educated, eternally sweet, polite, and clean?

The fourth difficulty derives from Homer's fictions which seem too far-fetched for us today, and too much outside the realm of verisimilitude we expect to live in. How can we ever bring our century to accept tripods walking on their own and even participating in assemblies? Or golden statues assisting Vulcan in his work? Or talking horses and many other fictitious inventions of that kind?

And, finally, the fifth difficulty, which has daunted me the most, is the grandeur, the nobility, and the harmony of diction nobody has ever come near to. It is not only beyond my own powers, but maybe even beyond those of our language itself.

All these causes for fear had greatly sapped my courage, but in the end I thought our ignorance of the nature of the epic, which has been with us for so long, has now been entirely dissipated by two excellent books which have been published on the matter. One is the *Treatise on Epic Poetry* written by the Reverend le Bossu, regular canon of Ste Geneviève, in which that learned religious scholar admirably elucidates the art of Homer's and Virgil's poems by applying Aristotle's rules to them. The other is the very *Poetics* of Aristotle himself, translated into French and enriched with commentaries which succeed admirably in making the reader sense how true and certain those rules are by bringing them to bear on his own reason and experience. I thought those two books had paved the way for my translation, so to speak, and that after such a wonderful explication of the rules I could venture to render into our language the very poems which constitute the examples on which those rules were based.

Some people say there is a better way to approach the original, which is to translate it into verse because, they add, poets must be translated into verse if all the ardor of poetry is to be preserved. There would surely be nothing better if such a thing were possible. But it is a mistake to think that this is the case, and it can be proved to be a mistake, at least in my opinion. I dared to say so before in my preface to Anacreon, and since then I have been fully confirmed in my judgment by the lack of success encountered by many verse translations. They have not been successful, not because their authors were not talented enough, since some of them enjoy a good reputation they owe to poetry. Rather, they have not been successful because the thing in itself is impossible, and rational arguments can be adduced as to why it should be so.

A translator can say in prose whatever Homer did say, but he can never do so in verse, certainly not in our language in which he must of necessity change, add, and cut. And what Homer thought and said is certainly of more value than all you are forced to put into his mouth if you translate him into verse, even if it comes out more simply and less poetic in prose.

That is the first reason. There is another, and I have already explained it: our poetry is unable to render all the beauty of Homer and to reach the heights he reached. It will be able to follow him in a few selected aspects. It will catch two, four, perhaps six lines. But in the end the texture will be so weak that the result will be utterly flaccid. And what is worse than cold and flaccid poetry, especially since all that falls short of excellence in poetry turns out to be unbearable?

When I speak of a prose translation I don't mean a servile translation. What I mean is a generous translation, a noble translation that clings closely to the ideas of its original, tries to match the beauty of its language, and renders its images without undue austerity of expression. The first type of translation, the servile one, becomes very unfaithful because it tries to be scrupulously faithful. It ruins the spirit by trying to save the letter. It is the work of a cold and sterile talent. The second type of translation, on the other hand, which tries above all to save the spirit, does not fail to keep the letter, even where it takes the greatest liberties. With its daring features, which remain true always, it becomes not just the faithful copy of its original, but a second original in its own right. It can only be the work of a writer of genius: solid, noble, and productive.

What I say here is said mainly to enlighten certain people who tend to have a very unflattering and highly erroneous idea of what translations are, mainly because they are almost totally ignorant of the nature and beauty of the Classics. They imagine translation to be a servile imitation in which the flowering of the spirit and the imagination have no part to play. In a word, they think translation is not creative. That is surely an immense mistake. A translation is not a copy of a painting in which the copier is willing to follow the lines, the proportions, the shapes, the attitudes of the original he imitates. A translation is entirely different: a good translator does not work under such constraints. At most he is like a sculptor who tries to recreate the work of a painter, or like a painter who tries to recreate the work of a sculptor. He is like Virgil who describes Lacoon according to the marble original, the admirable creation he could see before his eyes. In this imitation, as in all others, the soul must be filled with the beauty it wants to imitate. It must be intoxicated with the joyful exhalations emerging from those fertile sources and it must allow itself to be caught and transported by that strange enthusiasm. It must then proceed to make that enthusiasm its own and, in doing so, it must produce images and expressions that are quite different, even if they are similar. Maybe I can make all this clearer if I make use of a comparison taken from music. The world is full of musicians who are very learned in their art and sing exactly and rigorously all the notes of the songs they are presented with. They do not make a single mistake since they are cold and lack talent and fail to grasp the spirit in which these songs have been composed. Therefore they can put neither the grace in them, nor the joy that is their soul, as it were. But there are other musicians too, more alert and gifted with a more propitious talent, who sing those songs in the spirit in which they were composed, who safeguard all their beauty and make them appear very different, even though they are the same. And that is exactly the difference between good and bad translations, unless I am very much mistaken. Bad translations render the letter without the spirit in a low and servile imitation. Good translations keep the spirit without moving away from the letter. They are free and noble imitations that turn the familiar into something new.

Chapter 1

The role of ideology in the shaping of a translation

Translations are not made in a vacuum. Translators function in a given culture at a given time. The way they understand themselves and their culture is one of the factors that may influence the way in which they translate.

When Horace, for instance, speaks of a "faithful translator," he has the person in mind, much more so than the work that person produces. Translators, in Horace's understanding, thrive on the trust their patron and their public put in them. They do not have to translate "word for word" because both patron and audience literally "take their word" at face value.

Victor Hugo describes the other extreme: "When you offer a translation to a nation, that nation will almost always look on the translation as an act of violence against itself." Translations can be potentially threatening precisely because they confront the receiving culture with another, different way of looking at life and society, a way that can be seen as potentially subversive, and must therefore be kept out. Luther describes a successful attempt at ideological control when he accuses a "scribbler" of stealing his New Testament and goes on to say: "his prince, in a terrible preface, forbade the reading of Luther's New Testament and ordered the scribbler's New Testament read."

Ideology is often enforced by the patrons, the people or institutions who commission or publish translations.

Quintus Horatius, Flaccus, 65–8 BC. Roman poet.

Extract from the *Epistula ad Pisones* ("Letter to the Pisones"), also known as the *Ars Poetica*. Its exact date is unknown. It is usually dated around 10 BC.

Do not worry about rendering word for word, faithful translator, but render sense for sense.

Aurelius Augustinus, 354–430. Church father, theologian, writer.

Extract from *De doctrina christiana* ("On the Christian Doctrine"), written from 397–428.

Knowledge of foreign languages is necessary because translations of the same text tend to differ from each other, as I said before. The number of people who were able to translate the scriptures from Hebrew into Greek can easily be counted, but those who translated them from Greek into Latin are without number. When anybody stumbled on a Greek manuscript in the first days of the faith, he would begin to translate it even if he thought his command of both languages was limited.

The real sense, which many translators try to express according to their personal judgment and ability, is not firmly established when it is not established in the original language, since a translator very often misses the real sense when he is not very learned. That is why you should try to learn the languages from which the scriptures were translated into Latin, or you should at least stick to the work of such translators who have rendered their own original word for word. Such literal translations are insufficient, of course, but they can serve to show whether or not the translations of those who want to translate more according to the sense than according to the way the words are phrased are correct or not. For often not just individual words are translated, but also syntactical features that are simply not acceptable in Latin usage, if one wants to preserve the traditional style used by Latin writers up to now. Such a literal translation is often not exactly a hindrance to understanding, but it does irritate those readers who enjoy the content more when its verbal expression has managed to preserve a certain purity.

Extract from the "Letter to Saint Jerome," probably written in 392.

When one of our brothers, a bishop, had introduced the use of your translation in the church of which he is the pastor, the congregation hit upon a passage in the prophet Jonah which you translated in a very different way from the way it had established itself in the mind and memory of all, and the way it had been sung for such a long time. Great unrest arose among the people, especially since the Greeks protested and began to shout about falsification in a vituperative manner. As a result the bishop – it happened in the town of Onea – saw himself forced to rely on the Jews who lived in the city to clear up the matter. But they replied, either out of ignorance or out of malice, that the Hebrew manuscripts contained exactly what was also to be found in the Greek and Latin manuscripts. And then what? To escape from great danger the man was forced to correct himself, as if he had made a mistake, since he did not want to lose all the people in his church.

Martin Luther, 1483–1546. German theologian, polemicist, social thinker, and translator. Credited with setting off the Reformation by means of his translation of the New Testament.

Extract from his *Sendbrief vom Dolmetschen* ("Circular Letter on Translation"), published in 1530.

There has been much talk about the translation of the New Testament and half of the Old. The enemies of truth pretend that the text has been changed or even falsified in many places. Therefore many simple Christians, including the learned who do not know Hebrew or Greek, are overcome by fear and terror.

We are aware of the scribbler in Dresden who stole my New Testament. He admitted that my German is good and sweet and he realized that he could not do better, and yet he wanted to discredit it. So he took my New Testament as I wrote it, almost word for word, and he took my preface, my glosses, and my name away and wrote his name, his preface, and his glosses in their place. He is now selling my New Testament under his name. Oh, dear children, how hurt I was when his prince, in a terrible preface, forbade the reading of Luther's New Testament but ordered the scribbler's New Testament read, which is exactly the same as the one Luther wrote.

I have not taken a penny for it, I have not looked for one and I have not earned one.

Schlegel, August Wilhelm, 1767–1845. German critic, translator, and historian of literature.

Extract from *Geschichte der romantischen Literatur* ("History of Romantic Literature"), 1803.

Yet what I have just praised as an advantage, namely diligence and skill in translating, is rejected by many as an erroneous habit. They say that it originates in mental sluggishness and servility, and that it leads to more of the same, to the point of rendering you incapable of personal creation and invention. As opposed to this, it is easy to demonstrate that objective poetic translation is true writing, a new creation. Or if it is maintained that you should not translate at all, you would have to reply that the human mind hardly does anything else, that the sum total of its activity consists of precisely that. But it would carry us too far to develop this point here. Suffice it to say that higher artistic recreation has a nobler aim than the common craftsmanship of translation which exists only to remedy literary indigence. Its aim is nothing less than to combine the merits of all different nations, to think with them and feel with them, and so to create a cosmopolitan center for mankind.

Anne Louise Germaine de Staël, 1766–1817. French novelist, social and cultural critic, and writer of travelogues.

Extract from *Mélanges* (Writings), 1820.

The most eminent service one can render to literature is to transport the masterpieces of the human spirit from one language into another.

The best way to do without translations, I admit, would be to know all the languages in which the works of the great poets have been written: Greek, Latin, Italian, French, English, Spanish, Portuguese, German. But to do that you would need a lot of time and a lot of help and then you could never flatter yourself with the thought that knowledge so hard to acquire would, in fact, be acquired by all.

If translations of poems enrich literature, translations of plays could exert an even greater influence, for the theater is truly literature's executive power.

Victor Hugo, 1802–1885. French novelist, poet, dramatist.

Extract from the preface he wrote for the Shakespeare translations published by his son, François-Victor, in 1865.

When you offer a translation to a nation, that nation will almost always look on the translation as an act of violence against itself. Bourgeois taste tends to resist the universal spirit.

To translate a foreign writer is to add to your own national poetry; such a widening of the horizon does not please those who profit from it, at least not in the beginning. The first reaction is one of rebellion. If a foreign idiom is transplanted into a language in this way, that language will do all it can to reject that foreign idiom. This kind of taste is repugnant to it. These unusual locutions, these unexpected turns of phrase, that savage corruption of well-known figures of speech, they all amount to an invasion. What, then, will become of one's own literature? Who could ever dare think of infusing the substance of another people into its own very life-blood? This kind of poetry is excessive. There is an abuse of images, a profusion of metaphors, a violation of frontiers, a forced introduction of the cosmopolitan into local taste.

Chapter 2

The power of patronage

Translators tend to have relatively little freedom in their dealing with patrons, at least if they want to have their translations published.

John of Trevisa's "Lord" states quite unequivocally: "I would have a skilful translation, that might be known and understood," thus effectively delimiting the parameters for the translator's work. The Lord's answer to the translator's question: "Whether it is you liefer have, a translation of these chronicles in rhyme or in prose?" is equally obvious.

Patrons can encourage the publication of translations they consider acceptable and they can also quite effectively prevent the publication of translations they do not consider so. Jean de Brèche de Tours, for instance, is quite aware of the fact that his translation of Hippocrates will attract the "anger and mockery of many who seem to be eager to keep the sciences hidden from the people." His sentiments are echoed by Philemon Holland in the preface to his translation of Pliny.

Du Bellay provides perhaps the bluntest statement of the limitations of the translator's freedom: "the obedience one owes [to patrons] admits of no excuse." Publishers have since taken the place of Du Bellay's "princes and great lords," and they tend to operate in less draconian ways, but their influence on the shaping of translations should not be underestimated.

John of Trevisa, 1362–1412. English translator.

Extract from the "Dialogue between a Lord and a Clerk upon Translation," the preface to his translation of the *Polychronicon*, published in 1387.

The Clerk: Ye can speak, read, and understand Latin; then it needeth not have an English translation.

The Lord: I deny this argument; for though I can speak, read, and understand Latin, there is such Latin in those books that I cannot understand, neither thou, without studying, avisement, and looking of other books. Also, though it were not needful for me, it is needful for other men that understandeth no Latin.

The Clerk: Men that understand no Latin may learn and understand.

The Lord: Not all; for some may not for other manner business, some for age, some for default of wit, some for default of chattel, others of friends to find them to school, and some for other divers faults and lets.

The Clerk: Then they that understand no Latin may ask and be informed and ytaught of them that understand Latin.

The Lord: Thou speakest wonderly, for the lewd man wots not what he should ask, and namely of lore of deeds that come never in his mind; nor wots of whom commonly he should ask. Also, not all men that understand Latin have such books to inform lewd men; also some can not, and some may not, have while, and so it needeth to have an English translation.

The Clerk: The Latin is both good and fair, therefore it needeth not have an English translation.

The Lord: The reason is worthy to be plunged in a puddle and laid in a powder of lewdness and of shame. It might well be that thou makest only in mirth and in game.

The Clerk: The reason must stand but it be assoiled.

The Lord: Also holy writ in Latin is both good and fair, and yet for to make a sermon of holy writ all in Latin to

men that can English and no Latin, it were a lewd
deed, for they be never the wiser for the Latin, but
it be told them in English what the Latin is to mean
without translation out of Latin into English.
Then it needeth to have an English translation,
and for to keep it in mind that it be not forgeten, it
is better that such a translation be made and
written than said and not written. And so this
foresaid lewd reason should move no man that
hath any wit to leave the making of English translation.

The Clerk: If a translation were made that might be amended
in any point, some men it would blame.

The Lord: If men blame that is not worthy to be blamed, then
they be to blame. Clerks know well enough that no
sinful man doth so well that it ne might do better
ne make so good a translation that he ne be better.
I desire not translation of these the best that might
be, for that were an idle desire for any man that is
now alive, but I would have a skilful translation,
that might be known and understood.

The Clerk: Whether it is you liefer have, a translation of these
chronicles in rhyme or in prose?

The Lord: In prose, for commonly prose is more clear than
rhyme, more easy and more plain to know and
understand.

Jean de Brèche, called de Tours, 1514–c.1583. French
lawyer and translator.

Extract from the preface to his translation of
Hippocrates, published in 1555.

The translator, a learned man and an expert in languages, has
done his best to render into French the *Aphorisms* of Hippocrates
. . . even though he foresees that his labor may incur the anger
and mockery of many who seem to be eager to keep the sciences
hidden from the people.

Joachim Du Bellay, 1522–1560. French poet, literary theorist, and (auto)translator.

Extracts from the *Défense et illustration de la langue française*, published in 1549.

But what shall I say about those who really deserve to be called traitors, rather than translators, since they betray the authors they try to make known, robbing them of their glory and, at the same time, seducing ignorant readers by showing them black instead of white? To acquire the reputation of men of science they translate from languages they do not even know the first words of, such as Hebrew and Greek, and to increase that reputation they take on poets, the kind of writers I would never even get involved with if I could translate, or wanted to, because they possess the divine power of invention to a greater extent than other writers do. They have a grandeur of style, a magnificence of words, a weight to their sentences, an audacity and variety of figures of speech, and a thousand other highlights of poetry – in short, that ineffable spirit that pervades their writings. The Romans used to call it *genius*.

What I say is not meant for those who, at the command of princes and other great lords, translate the most famous Greek and Latin writers, since the obedience one owes those persons admits of no excuse in these matters.

Philemon Holland, 1552–1637. English scholar and translator.

Extract from "The Preface to the Reader" prefacing his translation of *The Historie of the World, Commonly Called The Natural Historie of C. Plinius Secundus*, 1634.

And yet some there be so gross to give out that these and such like books ought not to be published in the vulgar tongue. It is a shame (quoth one) that *Livy* speaketh English as he doth: Latinists only are to be acquainted with him: as who would say, the soldier were to have recourse unto the university for military skill and knowledge: or the scholar to put on arms and pitch a camp. What should *Pliny* (saith another) be read in English, and the mysteries couched in his books divulged: as if the husbandman, the mason, carpenter, goldsmith, painter, lapidary, and engraver, with other artificers, were bound to seek unto great clerks or linguists for instructions in their several arts. Certes, such *Momi*, or critics as these, besides their blind and erroneous opinion, think not so honourably of their native country and mother tongue as they ought: who if they were so well affected that way as they should be, would wish rather, and endeavour by all means to triumph now over the Romans in subduing their literature under the dent of the English pen, in requitall for the conquest sometime over this Island, achieved by the edge of their sword. As for our speech, was not Latin as common and natural in Italy, as English here with us. And if *Pliny* faulted not but deserved well of the Roman name, in laying abroad the riches and hidden treasures of Nature in that Dialect or Idiom which was familiar to the basest clown; why should any man be blamed for enterprising the semblable, to the commodity of that country in which and for which he was born. Are we the only nation under heaven unworthy to taste of such knowledge? or is our language so barbarous, that it will not admit in proper terms a foreign phrase?

I honour them in my heart who have of late days trodden the way before me in *Plutarch, Tacitus,* and others, have made good proof, that as the tongue in an Englishman's head is framed so flexible and obsequent, that it can pronounce naturally any other language; so a pen in his hand is able to sufficiently express Greek, Latin, and Hebrew. If myself, a man by profession otherwise carried away, for gifts far inferior to many, and wanting such helps as others be furnished with, have in some sort taught those to speak English who were supposed very untoward to be brought unto it; what may be expected at their hand, who for leisure may attend better; in wit are more pregnant; and being graced with the opinion of men and favour of the time, may attempt what they will, and effect whatsoever they attempt with greater felicity? A painful and tedious travail I confess it is; neither make I doubt but many do note me for much folly in spending time herein, and neglecting some compendious course of gathering good, and pursing up pence. But when I look back at the example of *Pliny*, I must of necessity condemn both mine own sloth, and also reprove the supine negligence of these days.

John Dryden, 1631–1700. English poet, dramatist, critic, and translator.

Extract from the "Dedication" to his translation of the *Aeneid*.

We are bound to our author's sense, though with the latitudes already mentioned; for I think it not so sacred, as that one iota must not be added or diminished, on pain of an *Anathema*. But slaves we are, and labor in another man's plantation; we dress the vineyard, but the wine is the owner's: if the soil be sometimes barren, then we are sure of being scourged: if it be fruitful, and our care succeeds, we are not thanked; for the proud reader will only say, the poor drudge has done his duty. But this is nothing to what follows; for, being obliged to make his sense intelligible, we are forced to untune our own verses, that we may give his meaning to the reader. He, who invents, is master of his thoughts and words: he can turn and vary them as he pleases, till he renders them harmonious; but the wretched translator has no such privilege: for, being tied to the thoughts, he must make what music he can in the expression; and, for this reason, it cannot always be so sweet as that of the original.

Johann Wolfgang von Goethe, 1749–1832. German poet, dramatist, novelist, critic.

Extract from the *Schriften zur Literatur* ("Writings on Literature"), 1824.

If we are able to put ourselves directly into such a distant situation, with no knowledge of local color and no understanding of the language, if we can observe a foreign literature at our ease, without having to do historical research, if we can bring the taste of a certain time to mind, the meaning of a nation and its genius, we must thank the translator who has exercised his talents for our benefit with great diligence, his whole life long.

A truly general tolerance will most certainly be reached if we respect the particular characteristics of single individuals and nations. We should, however, keep in mind that what has real merit distinguishes itself in that it belongs to humanity as a whole, and translate accordingly. Germans have contributed to such mediation and mutual recognition. Those who understand and study German find themselves on the market place where all nations offer their wares. They act as interpreters by enriching themselves.

That is how we should look upon every translator: he is a man who tries to be a mediator in this general spiritual commerce and who has chosen it as his calling to advance the interchange. Whatever you may say about the deficiencies of translation, it is and remains one of the most important and dignified enterprises in the general commerce of the world. The Qur'an says: "God has given every nation a prophet in its own language." Every translator is a prophet among his own people. The impact of Luther's Bible translation has been enormous, even though critics still find fault with it and express their reservations about it to this very day.

Chapter 3

Poetics

Etienne Dolet advises the translator to "link and arrange words with such sweetness that the soul is satisfied and the ears are pleased." Accordingly, translators often try to recast the original in terms of the poetics of their own culture, simply to make it pleasing to the new audience and, in doing so, to ensure that the translation will actually be read.

Few would go as far as Antoine Houdar de la Motte, who reduced the twenty-four books of the *Iliad* to twelve in his translation, not only for reasons of propriety – he left out the "anatomical details of wounds" – but also because he read the original in terms of the genre that dominated the poetics of his time: the tragedy. He therefore feels quite justified in asking: "Would a theater audience accept having characters come out during the intervals in a tragedy to tell us all that is going to happen next?" Consequently, he cuts all the passages in the *Iliad* where this can be said to happen.

Translators not infrequently use their translations to influence the evolution of the poetics of their time. Schlegel, for instance, objects to the fact that "our best dramatic works were written completely with French models in mind," and prescribes Shakespeare as an antidote for the German theater. The compromises translators find between the poetics of the original and the poetics of their culture provide fascinating insights into the process of acculturation and incontrovertible evidence of the extent of the power of a given poetics.

Etienne Dolet, 1509–1546. French poet, translator, printer, and publisher. Burnt at the stake because his translation of Plato contained some errors. Proof negative of the importance of patronage.

Extracts from *De la manière de bien traduire d'une langue en autre* ("On the Way of Translating Well from One Language into Another"), published in 1540.

First, the translator must understand to perfection the meaning and the subject matter of the author he translates. If he understands this he will never be obscure in his translation and if the author he translates is in no way obscene, he will be able to make him easily and perfectly intelligible.

The second point required in translation is that the translator should know the language of the author he translates to perfection and that he should have achieved the same excellence in the language he wants to translate into. In that way he will neither violate nor denigrate the splendor of one language or the other. You must understand that every language has its own characteristics, and therefore its diction, its patterns of speech, its subtleties, and its power must be translated accordingly. If the translator does not know this, he will hurt the author he translates and also the language he translates him into, for he will neither represent nor express the dignity and the riches of the two languages he has taken in hand.

The third point is that when you translate you should not enter into slavery to the point of rendering word for word. Whoever translates in this way does so because his mind is poor and deficient. If he possesses the qualities mentioned above (and a good translator must possess them) he will work with sentences and not care about the order of the words, and he will see to it that the author's intention is expressed while miraculously preserving the characteristics of both languages. It is therefore wrong to believe (should I call that belief stupidity or ignorance?) that you should start your translation at the beginning of a sentence. But if you express the intention of the author you translate you will be above reproach, even if you distort the syntax. I shall not pass over in silence the folly of some translators who bow to servitude instead of acting freely. They are such fools that they try to render line by line, or verse by verse. When they make this mistake they often adulterate the meaning of the author they translate and convey neither the elegance nor the perfection of either language. You must guard against this vice with all your might, since all it demonstrates is the translator's ignorance.

The fourth rule I want to offer here must be observed with greater diligence in languages that have not yet become established in the field of art than in others. I would call the following languages not yet established in the field of art: French, Italian, Spanish, German, English, and other vulgar tongues. If you translate a Latin book into one of these languages (even into French), you should not usurp words which are too close to Latin or have been little used in the past. Be satisfied with common usage and do not foolishly introduce novelties spawned by curiosity which can only be called reprehensible. If you observe some translators doing so, do not imitate them, since their arrogance is not worth a thing and cannot be tolerated among the learned. But do not think I am telling you the translator should completely abstain from using words outside common usage, since it is well known that Greek or Latin are richer in diction than French. This often forces us to use rare words, but we should do so only in cases of dire need.

Let us now come to the fifth rule a good translator needs to observe. It is such an important rule that all compositions are heavy and unpleasant without it. What is it then? Merely that the translator should observe the figures of speech, namely that he should link and arrange words with such sweetness that the soul is satisfied and the ears are pleased. He should never object to harmony in language. And I would once again like to admonish the translator to observe the rules I have given. If he does not, he will not be able to write any remarkable composition whatsoever: his sentences will not sound serious and they will not achieve their legitimate weight, as required.

Antoine Houdar de la Motte, 1672–1731. French writer, critic, and translator.

Extract from the preface to his translation of the *Iliad*, published in 1714.

I have a double reply to my critics: I have followed those parts of the *Iliad* that seemed to me worth keeping, and I have taken the liberty of changing whatever I thought disagreeable. I am a translator in many parts and an original author in many others.

I consider myself a mere translator wherever I have only made slight changes. I have often had the temerity to go beyond this, however: I did cut out whole books, I did change the way matters were set forth, and I have even invented new material.

Length is one of the factors that have been detrimental to our French poets: our poets have been beset by the wrong idea of emulation, and they have thought they had to run a course as long as that of Homer and Virgil.

The other reason that should have led our epic poets to reduce the size of their poems is that our lines of verse tend to fall in too uniform a cadence, which is pleasing for a while, but tiresome in the end.

For these reasons I have reduced the twenty-four books of the *Iliad* to twelve, which are even shorter than Homer's. At first sight you might think that this could only be done at the expense of many important elements. But if you pause to reflect that repetitions make up more than one-sixth of the *Iliad*, and that the anatomical details of wounds and the warriors' long speeches make up a lot more, you will be right in thinking that it has been easy for me to shorten the poem without losing any important features of the plot. I flatter myself that I have done just that and I even think I have succeeded in bringing the essential parts of the action together in such a way that they form a better proportioned and more sensible whole than Homer's original.

I would not have had to correct anything in the *Iliad*, except for the fact that what is moving in the poem has been weakened by detailed preparations that rob the events of all their surprise value and lessen the impression they make, or if these moving passages had not been interrupted by long episodes centered around indifferent characters, so that the reader loses sight of the characters he wants to keep track of. I thought I had to remedy these two defects by suppressing the unnecessary preparations and by cutting down on the uninteresting episodes. Would a theater audience accept having characters come out during the intervals in a tragedy to tell us all that is going to happen next? Would it approve if the actions of the principal characters were interrupted by the business of the *confidants*? Certainly not.

I have, therefore, only corrected – as far as possible – those defects in the poem that have a shocking or boring effect, since those are unforgivable. I have left the gods their passions, but I have always tried to preserve their dignity. I have not deprived the heroes of their unjust pride, which often appears as "grandeur" to us, but I have deprived them of the avarice, the eagerness, and the greed with which they stoop to looting, since these faults would bring them down in our eyes.

I have tried to make the narrative move at a faster pace than Homer does: the descriptions are grander and less weighed down with trivia, the comparisons less frequent and more exact. I have taken out of the speeches whatever I thought might run counter to the passion they express, and I have tried to put into them that mixture of power and sense that guarantees the best possible effect. Finally, I have tried to ensure continuity of character since it is this point – which has become so well established in our time – to which the reader is most sensitive, and that also makes him the sternest judge.

Voltaire (François-Marie Arouet), 1694–1778. French philosopher, dramatist, historian, satirist, and translator.

Extract from a letter written to Anne Dacier in 1720.

I am convinced that we have two or three poets in France who would be able to translate Homer very well; but I am equally convinced that nobody will read them unless they soften and embellish almost everything because, Madame, you have to write for your own time, not for the past.

August Wilhelm Schlegel, 1767–1845. German critic, translator, and literary historian.

Extract from "Etwas über Wilhelm Shakespeare bei Gelegenheit Wilhelm Meisters" ("Something about William Shakespeare on the Occasion of Wilhelm Meister"), 1796.

Over thirty years ago a writer [Wieland], who seemed least destined to become a translator because of the fertility of his own mind but who later became a classic for us in this field as well, dared to undertake the Herculean labor of translating most of Shakespeare into German for the first time. That labor was all the more Herculean then, because there were fewer aids to learning the English language, and because not much had been done to explain this often difficult and occasionally quite unintelligible poet – not even in English.

[Wieland] was not immediately given the credit he deserved, and that is not surprising, because our theaters were still generally dominated by inspired imitations from the French, and even our best dramatic works were written completely with French models in mind. Who would have dared to imagine then that such pagan, unruly, and barbaric plays ascribed by obscure rumor to an Englishman, a certain William Shakespeare, would ever have been allowed to be shown before our eyes? Lessing, that valiant enemy of prejudice, was the first to reveal French tragic wit in its nakedness, and to emphatically defend Shakespeare's merit. He also reminded the Germans that they possessed a translation of that great poet, and that they would be able to learn from it for a long time before they would need a new one, even if the translation they had was not perfect.

To be sure he could not have foreseen what happened a few years later. The style of his own dramatic works, especially *Emilia Galotti*, helped to make his fellow citizens more receptive to Shakespeare. Together with a few other factors, the publication of *Goetz von Berlichingen* was to usher in a whole new epoch in our theaters, for better or for worse. Not long before that, only the Englishman had been praised with a glowing eloquence that would silence his opponents even if it failed to convince them, and the truth was impressed upon us all that the entire set of rules regulating fashionable refinement simply could not be used as a yardstick to measure his creations. Only nine years after the publication of Wieland's translation the need was felt, not for a reprint, but for a better Germanization of all of Shakespeare's works. Since Wieland himself could not undertake the task it fortunately fell to one of our most learned and most discerning men of letters [Johann Joachim Eschenburg], whose sound knowledge of the language, uncommon ingenuity in explication, and assiduous care gave the translation what it had been lacking until then: overall completeness and precision of detail.

Even though the knowledge of English has spread widely in Germany, it very rarely reaches the level required if one is not to be continuously interrupted in one's pleasure, or even scared away from reading the poet altogether. How few are there among those who can read him in his entirety (that is to say, those passages excepted where the English themselves need a commentary because the words have become obsolete, the allusions unknown, or the texts corrupt) without interruption – how few are those who can feel and recognize all the more refined beauty, the tender nuances of expression on which the harmony of poetic representation rests, with a facility equal to the one they possess in their mother tongue? How few have mastered English pronunciation to the extent that they can read the poet aloud with the required euphony and emphasis? Yet all of this greatly increases his impact, since poetry is obviously not a silent art. Readers of Shakespeare who have passed all the tests described above would, moreover, not be adverse to relaxing on their own turf now and then, for a change, in the shadow of his works, so to speak, provided those works could be transplanted without too great a loss of their beautiful foliage. Would it not be a good thing, therefore, if we had a translation? "But we have one already, and it is complete, faithful, and good." So it is! We had to have that much to be able to wish for more. The desire for luxury follows the satisfaction of basic needs. Now the best is no longer good enough for us. If Shakespeare could and should be translated only into prose we ought to remain satisfied with what has been achieved so far. But he is a poet, also in the very connection of his words to the use of meter. If it were possible to recreate his work faithfully and poetically at the same time, if it were possible to follow the letter of his meaning step by step and yet to capture some of the innumerable, indescribable marvels that do not reside in the letter, but float above it like a breath of spirit! It would be well worth the effort.

Edward Fitzgerald, 1809–1883. English translator and poet.

Extract from the preface to his *Rubaiyat of Omar Khayyam*, 1859.

The original Rubaiyat (as, missing an Arabic Guttural, these *Tetrastichs* are more musically called) are independent stanzas, consisting of four lines of equal, though varied prosody, sometimes *all* rhyming, but oftener (as here attempted) the third line suspending the Cadence by which the last atunes with the former two. Something as in the Greek Alcaic, where the third line seems to lift and suspend the wave that falls over the last. As usual with such kind of Oriental Verse, the Rubaiyat follow one another according to Alphabetic Rhyme — a strange Farrago of Grave and Gay. Those here selected are strung into something of an Eclogue, with perhaps a less than equal proportion of the "Drink and make merry," which (genuine or not) recurs over-frequently in the Original.

Ulrich von Willamowitz-Moellendorff, 1848–1931. German philologist and translator.

Extract from "Die Kunst des Übersetzens" ("The Art of Translation"), 1924.

Everyone should know by now that this whole direction [of metrical translation] is wrong, that it goes against the very nature of language, because the Germanic languages, or rather all contemporary European languages, do not have long and short, but stressed and unstressed syllables. Poets have, in fact, abandoned that direction by now, and only the hexameter and the distichon, with perhaps a couple of meters taken from the odes, are still put to use occasionally, though not a single one of them has become popular.

But how should we render the poetry of antiquity? One thing must be stated first: Homer is untranslatable because we do not have an epic meter, because we do not write stories in verse. Any meter that is even slightly stanzaic disrupts the free movement of the Homeric story, and a pair of rhymes already amounts to a distichon. But the style, too, is inimitable because of its ornamental words and because it is formulaic in many respects. Homer is not popular poetry but definitely the poetry of high art. A Homer in prose must divest himself of his jewels, in other words lose all the color of life. The dialogue of Greek drama stands a better chance, because in this case we have our classical style and a verse form that can be modified to suit comedy as well, even if we still have to find a poet who can do this for Menander. As to the epigram, one could take Goethe's distichs (rarely, I believe), but they are of no use for the Greek elegy, nor for Propertius, for instance, because they are Ovidic. And no rules at all can be given for all the poetry that was sung, for all lyrical poetry, and for the Hellenistic and Roman poetry that belongs to high art. Whoever wants to try them should, in any case, look for a German form analogous to the original in mood and style. Let him decide to what extent he can adapt himself to the form of the original. His intention as a translator will be a decisive factor, as will be his understanding of the text.

We are faced with a totally different matter when a creative poet takes up an ancient work and transforms it recreatively in his own spirit. This is quite legitimate, even great, but it is not a translation. For translation only wants to let the ancient poet speak to us clearly and in a manner as immediately intelligible as he did in his own time. He must be given words, he must speak through our mouth. "True translation is metempsychosis." This implies that the ancient poet, whose own lines lead an immortal life, must time and again cast his spirit on a new translator, because translations are mortal, indeed even short-lived. And if an old philologist who has often tried his hand at this is to say how it should be done, he can suggest how it should not be done, but for the rest he will know better than to give recipes. Necessary though it is, learning is not sufficient, not even to understand the text, and when translation is also something like the writing of poetry the Muse's help is most definitely needed.

Chapter 4

Universe of Discourse

In the introduction to his translation of Lucian, Perrot d'Ablancourt explains why he left out certain passages in the original: "All comparisons dealing with love speak of the love of boys, a custom not strange among the Greeks, even though it seems horrible to us." Translators have to strike a balance between the Universe of Discourse (i.e. the whole complex of concepts, ideologies, persons, and objects belonging to a particular culture) as acceptable to the author of the original, and that other Universe of Discourse which is acceptable and familiar to the translator and his or her audience. It happens not infrequently that translators decide, with le Tourneur, that foreign authors are "not always models of taste," resolving, therefore, to "assimilate all that is good in our neighbors and reject the bad we have no need to read or know of."

In most cases translators do not reject outright, but rather rewrite, both on the level of content and on the level of style since, as the Earl of Roscommon observes: "Words in one language eloquently used/ Will hardly in another be excused." "Fidelity" in translation can therefore be shown to be not just, or even not primarily a matter of matching on the linguistic level. Rather, it involves a complex network of decisions to be made by translators on the level of ideology, poetics, and Universe of Discourse.

Nicolas Perrot d'Ablancourt, 1606–1664. French translator. His translations were the first to be graced with the epithet "belles infidèles" (beautiful but unfaithful).

Extract from the preface to his translation of Lucian, published in 1709.

Anyway, you can learn many remarkable things here, and the work is like a bouquet of flowers that contains what is most beautiful in the ancient writers. I only mention in passing that the stories have been told in such an ingenious way that they are hard to forget. This contributes greatly to the understanding of poets. You must therefore not think it strange that I have translated this work, following the example of many learned people who have produced Latin versions of this dialogue or that, and I am the less to blame in that I have left out what was too filthy and softened what was too free, at least in some places. This is how I justify my conduct, and the translation I attempted is justified by the many advantages that will come to the public from its reading of this author. I will only say that I have left him in the full vigor of his opinions, since I would not have produced a translation otherwise. But I comment on the strongest of these opinions in my introduction, or in the notes, so as to render them relatively harmless.

Since most of what is to be found here is said in jest and contains jokes that are different in all languages, a regular translation proved to be impossible to undertake. There are even passages in the book that have proved untranslatable because they depend completely on the intrinsic value of the Greek words and would not be understood beyond them. All comparisons dealing with love speak of the love of boys, a custom not strange among the Greeks, even though it seems horrible to us. The author keeps quoting lines from Homer. Doing so now would create the impression of pedantry. He also keeps quoting old hackneyed stories, proverbs, examples, and outworn comparisons sure to produce, in our time, an effect contrary to the author's intention, since we are dealing with jocularity here, not with erudition. I had to change all of this accordingly if I wanted to produce something that is pleasing. It would not be Lucian if it were not, but what is pleasing in his language would not be bearable in ours. When you look at a beautiful face you will always discover some feature in it which you wish were not there. Similarly, the best authors contain passages that need to be touched up or clarified, certainly when the text has been written with the sole aim to please, since in that case you are not allowed to make even the slightest mistake, and if you are just a trifle indelicate you will bore your readers instead of entertaining them.

Consequently, I do not always stick to the author's words, nor even to his thoughts. I keep the effect he wanted to produce in mind, and then I arrange the material after the fashion of our time. Different times do not just require different words, but also different thoughts, and ambassadors usually dress in the fashion of the country they are sent to, for fear of appearing ridiculous in the eyes of the people they try to please.

What I have produced is certainly not a translation, properly speaking. It is better than a translation and the writers of classical antiquity did not translate otherwise. Terence treated the comedies he took from Menander in the same way even though Aulius Gellius insists on calling the end product a translation. What does it matter what we call the thing, as long as it exists? Cicero took the same course of action in his *Offices*, which are almost a version of Panetus, and also in the versions he made of the oratory of both Aeschines and Demosthenes. Cicero says he did not write as an interpreter, but as an orator, and I say the same about Lucian's *Dialogues* even though I have not allowed myself the same freedom in all cases. In fact, there are many passages I have translated word for word, at least to the extent to which that is possible in an elegant translation. There are also passages in which I have considered what ought to be said, or what I could say, rather than what he actually said. In this I have followed the example set by Virgil in his borrowings from Homer and Theocritus, and I have pointed out what I was doing almost everywhere, without lapsing into particulars, since that is no longer done in our time. I am fully convinced, however, that not everybody will be satisfied with my way of doing things and that those who idolize every single word and every single thought produced by the writers of antiquity will be most displeased, as is invariably the case with people who think a work of literature cannot be good as long as its author is still alive.

Jacques Delille, 1738–1813. French cleric, poet, and translator.

Extract from the preface to his translation of Virgil's *Georgics*, published in 1769.

I have always thought of translation as a way to enrich a language. If you write an original work in a particular language you are likely to exhaust that language's own resources, if I may say so. If you translate, you import the riches contained in foreign languages into your own, by means of felicitous commerce.

I have chosen to translate in verse, since a translation of verse into prose is always an unfaithful one. There are those who maintain that even the best translation in verse disfigures the original and dilutes its beauty. I merely refer them to the translation the famous Mr. Pope made of Homer, or to the translation of Virgil made by Mr. Dryden, which allows us to get to know Virgil better than the best prose version does. At least we have a poet translating a poet.

I shall explain the system of translation I have followed, the liberties I have taken. I have always maintained that extreme faithfulness in translation results in extreme unfaithfulness. A word may be noble in Latin and its French equivalent may be base. If you insist on extreme faithfulness you will replace a noble style with a base one. Alternatively, a Latin expression may be strong and precise and you may need more than one word to render it into French. If you are faithful you will be long-winded. An expression that is bold in Latin may be trenchant in French and you will end up replacing boldness with insensitivity. A sequence of words may be harmonious in the original but the words that correspond to them in the translation may not be as melodious. Harmony will be replaced by discord. If an image was new in the Latin writer but has become worn out in French, you will find yourself replacing a new image with a trivial one. Finally, a geographical detail or an allusion to a custom may have been pleasing to the people your author wrote for. It may no longer be so to your reader. You will merely be strange where your author was interesting.

So what is the skillful translator to do? He studies the nature of both languages. He is faithful where they do not deviate and where they do he fills the gap with an equivalent that safeguards the rights of his own language while following the author's genius as closely as possible. Every writer has his own physiognomy and his own gait, so to speak. He can be more or less warm, more or less ingenious, more or less quick. The translator should therefore not resort to Ovid's brilliant, fecund, and diffuse style to render Virgil who is always simple and precise.

But the translator's most essential duty, the one that crowns all others, is to try to reproduce the effect the author produced, in every instance. He must be able to produce the same beautiful passages, as far as possible, or at least the same number of beautiful passages. Whoever wants to translate goes into debt. To repay it he must pay the same sum but not in the same currency. If he is unable to render the image he should replace it with a thought. If he cannot paint for the ear he should paint for the mind. If he is less energetic he should be more harmonious and he should be richer if he is less precise. Does he foresee that he will have to weaken his author in a certain passage? Let him strengthen that author in another. Let him give back below what he takes away above. Let him compensate everywhere while staying as close as possible to the nature of the original in all its parts. For this reason it is unjust to compare each one of the translator's lines with the corresponding line in the original. His merit must be determined on the basis of the totality of his work and the overall effect produced by every passage.

Pierre le Tourneur, 1736–1788. French translator, especially of Young and Shakespeare.

Extract from the preface to his translation of Young's *Night Thoughts*, published in 1769.

It has been my intention to distill from the English Young a French one to be read with pleasure and interest by French readers who would not have to ask themselves whether the book they were reading was a copy or an original. It seems to me that authors who write in foreign languages should be translated in this way since they are not always models of taste, even if their superior literary merit is not in doubt. If we translated this way we would assimilate all that is good in our neighbors and reject the bad we have no need to read or know of.

Antoine Prévost, better known as Abbé Prévost, 1697–1763. French novelist and translator.

Extract from the preface to his translation of Richardson's *Pamela*, published in 1760.

I have not changed anything pertaining to the author's intention, nor have I changed much in the manner in which he put that intention into words, and yet I have given his work a new face by ridding it of the flaccid excursions, the excessive descriptions, the useless conversations, and the misplaced musings. The main criticism addressed to Mr. Richardson is that he sometimes loses sight of the main points of his work and drowns in details. I have fought a continuous battle against this lack of proportion that undermines the reader's interest. Should some trace of it have survived I must admit that such is inevitable in a story that is told by means of an exchange of letters. I have suppressed English customs where they may appear shocking to other nations, or made them conform to customs prevalent in the rest of Europe. It seemed to me that those remainders of the old and uncouth British ways, which only habit prevents the British themselves from noticing, would dishonor a book in which manners should be noble and virtuous. To give the reader an accurate idea of my work, let me just say, in conclusion, that the seven volumes of the English edition, which would amount to fourteen volumes in my own, have been reduced to four.

Voltaire (François-Marie Arouet), 1694–1778. French philosopher, dramatist, historian, satirist, and translator.

Extracts from the preface to his translation of Shakespeare's *Julius Caesar*.

The reader will easily be able to compare Shakespeare's thoughts, his style, and his judgment with what Corneille has written and thought. Readers of all nations shall then sit in judgment over both, even though a Frenchman and an Englishman may be suspected of some partiality in the matter. To make this a fair trial I have to produce an exact translation. I put into prose what is prose in Shakespeare's tragedy and I used blank verse where Shakespeare uses it. What is lowly and familiar has been translated in the same way. I have tried to soar with the author where he soars and I have taken great care not to add or take away anything where he is turgid and bombastic.

John Hookham Frere, 1769–1846. British diplomat and translator. His translations of Pulci gave Byron the English *ottava rima* for *Don Juan*, a fact not usually recorded in literary histories.

Extracts from the preface to his translations of Aristophanes, published in 1840.

But even if the style of our own old comedies were suited to represent the character of the ancient Aristophanic comedy; which from the essential differences subsisting between the two genera, we think, that it is *not*; – and even supposing that ancient style to be perfectly imitated, we should still feel an objection, arising from the very perfection of the imitation; as it would have a constant tendency to destroy that illusion which it is the object of the translator to create: the translation might be admirable but the reader would be constantly reminded that he was reading an admirable translation – he would never be allowed to lose himself in the thoughts and images, and forget for a moment the language in which they were conveyed to him.

The language of translation ought, we think, as far as possible, to be a pure, impalpable and invisible element, the medium of thought and feeling, and nothing more; it ought never to attract attention to itself; hence all phrases that are remarkable in themselves, either as old or new, all importations from foreign languages, and quotations, are as far as possible to be avoided.

We think that licenses of this kind have in themselves a character of petulance and flippancy . . . they belong more properly to that class of translators who are denominated *Spirited Translators*, whose spirit and ability consist in substituting a modern variety or peculiarity for an ancient one, to the utter comfusion of all unity of time, place, and character; leaving the mind of the reader bewildered as in a masquerade, crowded and confused with ancient and modern costumes. Of this class of translators, and of their ancient and inveterate antagonists, the *Faithful Translators*, we should wish to say something, because we think that it may tend to illustrate the principle of translation generally. The proper domain of the Translator is, we conceive, to be found in that vast mass of feeling, passion, interest, action and habit which is common to mankind in all countries and in all ages; and which, in all languages, is invested with its appropriate forms of expression, capable of representing it in all its infinite varieties, in all the permanent distinctions of age, profession, and temperament which have remained immutable, and of which the identity is to be traced almost in every page of the author before us.

Nothing can be more convincing or more deeply astonishing than the result which must remain upon the mind of every man who has read the remains of Aristophanes with the attention which they deserve. It is evident that every shade of the human character, and the very mode in which each is manifested, remain the same; not a genius or a species is become extinct; many even which might naturally have been considered as mere accidental varieties, are still preserved, or have been reproduced.

*

The original author who is addressing his contemporaries must of course make use of phrases according to their conventional import; he will likewise, for the sake of immediate effect, convey his general observations in the form of local or even personal allusion. It is the office, we presume, of the Translator to represent the forms of language according to the intention with which they are deployed; he will therefore in his translation make use of the phrases in his own language to which habit and custom have assigned a similar conventional import, taking care, however, to avoid those which, from their form or any other circumstances, are connected with associations exclusively belonging to modern manners; he will likewise, if he is capable of executing his task upon a philosophic principle, endeavour to resolve the personal and local allusions into the genera, of which the local or personal variety employed by the original author is merely the accidental type; and to reproduce them in one of those permanent forms which are connected with the universal and immutable habits of mankind. The Faithful Translator will not venture to take liberties of this kind; he *renders* into English all the conversational phrases according to their grammatical and logical form, without any reference to the current usage which had affixed to them an arbitrary sense, and appropriated them to a particular and definite purpose. He retains scrupulously all the local and personal peculiarities, and in the most rapid and transient allusions thinks it his duty to arrest the attention of the reader with a tedious explanatory note. The Spirited Translator, on the contrary, employs the corresponding modern phrases; but he is apt to imagine that a peculiar liveliness and vivacity may be imparted to his performance by the employment of such phrases as are particularly connected with modern manners; and if at any time he feels more than usually anxious to avoid the appearance of pedantry, he thinks he cannot escape from it in any way more effectually than by adopting the slang and jargon of the day. The peculiarities of ancient times he endeavours to represent by substituting in their place the peculiarities of his own time and nation.

Dillon Wentworth, Earl of Roscommon, 1633–1685.
English translator and thinker on translation.

Extracts from his *Essay on Translated Verse*, published in 1685.

'Tis true, Composing is the Nobler Part,
But good Translation is no *easy* Art
For tho Materials have long since been found
Yet both your Fancy and your Hands are bound
And by Improving what was writ before,
Invention Labors less, but Judgment more.

The first great work (a Task perform'd by few)
Is that your self may to your self be True:
No Masque, no Tricks, no Favor, no Reserve;
Dissect your Mind, examine ev'ry Nerve.
Whoever vainly on his strength depends,
Begins like Virgil, but like Maevius ends:
That wretch, in spight of his forgotten Rhymes,
Condemn'd to Live to all succeeding Times.

Each Poet with a different Talent writes,
One praises, one instructs, another bites;
Horace did ne'er aspire to Epic Bays,
Nor lofty Maro stoop to Lyric Lays.
Examine how your Humor is inclin'd,
And which the Ruling Passion of your Mind;
Then seek a Poet who your way does bend,
And choose an Author as you choose a Friend:
United by this sympathetic Bond,
You grow familiar, intimate and fond;
Your Thoughts, your Words, your Styles, your Souls agree
No longer his interpreter, but he.

Immodest words admit of no defence,
For want of Decency is want of Sense.
What moderate Fop would rake the Park or Stews,
Who among Troops of faultless Nymphs may choose?
Variety of such is to be found;
Take then a Subject proper to expound:
But moral, great, and worth a Poet's Voice,
For Men of sense despise a trivial Choice:

And such applause it must expect to meet,
As would some painter, busy in a Street,
To copy Bulls and Bears and ev'ry Sign
That calls the staring Sots to nasty wine.
Yet 'tis not all to have a subject *good*;
It must delight us when 'tis understood.

Instruct the list'ning world how Maro sings
Of useful subjects and of lofty Things:
These will such true, such bright Ideas raise,
As merit Gratitude as well as Praise;
But foul Descriptions are offensive still,
Either for being like or being ill.
For who, without a Qualm, has ever looked
On Holy Garbage, though by Homer cooked?

Take pains the genuine Meaning to explore,
There sweat, there strain, tug the laborious Oar.
Search ev'ry Comment that your care can find,
Some here, some there may hit the Poet's Mind
Yet be not blindly guided by the Throng
The Multitude is always in the Wrong.
When things appear unnatural or hard,
Consult your Author, with Himself compar'd.

Truth still is One; Truth is divinely bright:
No cloudy Doubts obscure her native Light:
While in your Thoughts you find the least debate,
You may confound, but never can translate.
Your Style will this through all Disguises show,
For none explain more clearly than they know:
He only proves he understands a Text,
Whose Exposition leaves it unperplexed.

Words in one Language elegantly used
Will hardly in another be excused,
And some that Rome admired in Caesar's Time
May neither suit our Genius nor our Clime.
The genuine Sense, intelligibly told,
Shows a Translator both discreet and bold.
Excursions are inexpiably bad,
And 'tis much safer to leave out than add.
Abstruse and mystic thoughts you must express

With painful care but seeming easiness,
For truth shines brightest through the plainest dress.

I pity from my Soul unhappy Men
Compelled by Want to prostitute their Pen,
Who must, like Lawyers, either starve or plead,
And follow, right or wrong, where Guineas lead;
But you, Pompilian, wealthy, pampered Heirs,
Who to your Country owe your Swords and Cares,
Let no vain Hope your easy Mind seduce,
For rich ill Poets are without Excuse.
'Tis very Dangerous Tampring with a Muse:
The Profit's small, and you have much to lose;

Of many Faults Rhyme is perhaps the Cause;
Too strict to Rhyme, we slight more useful Laws;
For That in Greece or Rome was never known,
Till, by Barbarian Deluges o'erflown,
Subdued, undone, they did at last obey
And change their own for their Invaders' way.

Chapter 5

Translation, the development of language, and education

Juan Luis Vives quotes Quintilian with approval where the latter advises: "When we translate from Greek we should not follow that language in all things, especially not when they want to use their words to designate our things." Rather, if translators want to really translate items belonging to the original's Universe of Discourse that do not exist in their own, they will have to "coin new expressions," as Cicero advised. By doing so, translators have, over the centuries, enriched their native languages not only with new vocabulary but also, in Pliny's words, with an "abundance of stylistic figures and resources."

Nor do translators' contributions stop where the development of language as such is concerned. Pelletier du Mans remarks that translators "are, in part, the reason why France has at last been able to begin to taste good things" in the field of literature. Translation has also traditionally been considered the best school for creative writers, simply because, in Gottsched's words, it allows them to "make up a hundred little rules for themselves."

Translation as a pedagogical tool has traditionally not only been restricted to creative writers: generations of European schoolchildren have learned foreign languages by means of translation from about 100 AD until the end of World War Two in order to acquire a feel for the language in the domain where, as Schlegel remarks: "the grammarian's judicial functions cease."

Marcus Tullius Cicero, 106–43 BC. Roman orator, politician, and philosopher.

Extract from *De oratore* ("On the Orator"), dated 55 BC.

I decided to take speeches written in Greek by great orators and to translate them freely, and I obtained the following results: by giving a Latin form to the text I had read I could not only make use of the best expressions in common usage with us, but I could also coin new expressions, analogous to those used in Greek, and they were no less well received by our people as long as they seemed appropriate.

Extract from *De finibus bonorum et malorum* ("On the Limits of Good and Evil"), dated 44 BC.

Yet it will not be necessary to render the Greek term by means of a Latin word that is a calque of it, as is the custom of translators who do not know how to express themselves, when we already have a more common word that says the same thing. You could even do what I usually do: where the Greeks have one word I use more than one if I can't translate otherwise, but that does not mean that I should not have the right to use a Greek word whenever Latin is unable to offer an equivalent.

Marcus Fabius Quintilianus, 35–96. Roman orator, lawyer, and teacher.

Extract from the *Institutio oratoria* ("Guide to Rhetoric"), published in 96.

And the reason for this exercise is easy to find. The Greek authors are blessed with an abundance of ideas and they have put an infinity of art into their eloquence. When we translate we are allowed to avail ourselves of the best words, since all the words we use are our own. As for the figures of speech, those chief ornaments of discourse, we are also forced to imagine a great many of them and to vary them, since the way in which the Roman express themselves generally differs from that of the Greeks.

Hieronymus (Saint Jerome), 345–419/420. Church father, translator, historian, and polemicist.

Extract from the "Letter to Pammachius," probably written between 405 and 410.

I admit and confess most freely that I have not translated word for word in my translations of Greek texts, but sense for sense, except in the case of the scriptures in which even the order of the words is a mystery. Cicero has been my teacher in this.

Do Plautus and Terence, for example, stick to the word, or do they try to preserve the beauty and the elegance of the original in translation? Educated people have coined the phrase *kako zelia*, misplaced zeal for what you call a faithful translation. I have derived my principles from the writers I mentioned when I translated the chronicles of Eusebius into Latin twenty years ago. In your opinion I committed the same mistakes as they did but I never suspected that you would go on to blame me for them. In those days I wrote in my introduction, among other things:

> It is hard not to slip when you are translating a foreign text word for word. It is difficult to preserve the elegance of felicitous expression as you find it in a foreign language when you translate. Something may find its most poignant expression through the proper nature of *one* word. I cannot find the one that achieves the same effect. If I want to do justice to the sense I have to make a long detour to get just a little bit ahead. Add to this the irritating anacoluths, or sentences that do not make sense, the difference in cases, the multiplicity of images and, finally, the spirit that dwells in every language, your own and that of others. If I translate word for word I produce nonsense, but if I have to change something in the order of the words or their sound I could be accused of failing in my duties as a translator.

After a few more sentences that are of no interest to us here, I added: "If people maintain that the beauty of a language does not suffer from translation let them simply translate Homer into Latin, word for word, or even better, let them simply render him in prose in his own language. The whole thing will turn into a ridiculous comedy and the greatest poet will be reduced to a mere stammerer."

I only wanted to prove that I have always been opposed to sticking to words, from the days when I was young, and that I have always translated the sense. But my judgment is probably not of great importance in this matter. I advise people to read the short preface to the book that describes the life of Saint Antony. It says there:

> A literal translation from one language into another obscures the sense in the same way as the thriving weeds smother the seeds. Since language depends on cases and images you sometimes have to waste time and make a detour to express what could be said with few words, and often to express it with great imprecision at that. I have skirted this danger and at your

request I have translated the life of Saint Antony in such a way that the whole sense is there, even if I have not always kept to the sound of the words. Let others stick to syllables, or even to letters, you should try to grasp the sense!

It would lead us too far to point out how much the translators of the *Septuagint* have added and how much they have left out. In the manuscripts we use in our churches these passages are marked with small obelix and small asterisks. Yet the *Septuagint* has become the accepted translation in churches, and rightly so, not only because it was the first translation and because it was already in use before the coming of Christ, but also because it was used by the apostles, though only in as far as it did not deviate from Hebrew.

Roger Bacon, 1220–1292. English cleric, scientist, mathematician, and inventor. A "Renaissance man" about two centuries ahead of his time.

Extract from *De linguarum cognitio* ("On the Knowledge of Languages"), dated 1267.

I now want to deal with the science that is, at first sight, the most important one of all. The Holy Scriptures have been translated from Greek and Hebrew and philosophy has been translated from Arabic as well as from those two languages. Yet it is impossible to preserve the distinctive features of one language in another since even idiomatic expressions in the same language tend to differ among its speakers, as is obvious in French. Parisians, Picardians, Normans, and Burgundians use idioms in different ways. What is considered correct among Picardians tends to fill the Burgundians with horror, and the Parisians too, because they are closer to them. If this happens inside one language imagine the extent to which it happens between different languages. Consequently, what is well said in one language cannot possibly be transferred into another in the same way.

For this reason Hieronymus states the following in his epistle on the best way to translate: "If anybody thinks a language does not change in translation, let him try to translate Homer literally into Latin. If he then goes on to translate that translation into his own language he will see that the syntax is ridiculous and that the most eloquent of poets is hardly able to speak at all." Whoever knows a discipline, such as logic or any other, well, and tries to translate it into his mother tongue will discover that mother tongue lacking in both substance and words. Therefore no reader of Latin will be able to understand the wisdom contained in philosophy and in the Holy Scriptures as well as he should, unless he also knows the languages they have been translated from.

Juan Luis Vives, 1492–1540. Spanish humanist.

Extract from "Versiones seu Interpretationes" ("Versions or Translations"), published in 1531.

A version is the transfer of words from one language into another in such a way that the sense is preserved. In some versions you can see only the sense, in others only the phrasing and the diction. If a man wanted to transfer the speeches of Demosthenes or Marcus Tullius [Cicero], or the poems of Homer and Virgil into other languages, he would have to pay attention first and foremost to the way the text is put together and to the figures of speech it contains. If he did that he would soon realize how great the differences between languages are, if he had not already done so before, since no one language is rich enough to match another in all stylistic traits and figures of speech, even the most primitive ones. "When we translate from Greek we should not follow that language in all things," says Marcus Fabius [Quintilianus] "especially not when they want to use their words to designate our things." There is a third kind of text in which both the substance and the words are important, in which words bring power and elegance to the senses, so to speak, whether taken singly, in conjunction with other words, or in the text as a whole. Texts written with only the sense in mind should be translated freely and the translator should be allowed to omit what does not add to the sense, or to add what improves it. It is impossible to express the figures of speech and patterns characteristic of one language in another, even less so when they are idiomatic, and I fail to see what purpose would be served in admitting solecisms and barbarisms with the sole aim of representing the sense with as many words as are used in the original, the way some translations of Aristotle or Holy Writ have been made. It should be acceptable to render two words by means of one, or one word by means of two, or more as usage dictates, and to add words or to leave them out.

Translations are not merely advantageous to all the arts and sciences but absolutely vital to them, both for a whole life and for specific moments in it, as long as they are faithful to the original.

Translations tend to become unfaithful because translators do not know the language or the topic they are dealing with. Words are finite in number but things are infinite and therefore many people are taken in by the similarities between words, what is called synonymy, and they do not know what the text is about. Consequently, ignorant translators are deceived and deceive those who trust them, sometimes on the level of style and diction and sometimes on the level of content or that of the characteristic features an author uses. That is why you sometimes notice that those who translate Aristotle or Galen fail to do so successfully and fail to communicate the stature of the work because they do not know philosophy or medicine the way their author does. In these translations both word and thing, stylistic features and figures of speech need to be taken into account. Other ornaments in the text need to be preserved as far as possible according to the translator's ability. They need to be preserved with the same power and elegance in so far as those are compatible with the language of the translation. It is often possible only to render the power or the elegance, which constitute two different features in the original language.

Languages benefit greatly if skillful translators dare to give some foreign figure of speech or style to their nation, as long as it does not deviate too much from that nation's customs and general way of life. They can also imitate the language of the original, using it as a kind of matrix, and invent or construct new well-formed words to enrich the language they translate into.

Yet not everybody can allow himself to do that and it is wiser to be sparing and meticulous in these matters rather than foolhardy and overproductive. There are translations of the sense in which the words should also be considered very carefully so that they can be approximated, if possible, even in passages that are very difficult and hard to understand. Many of Aristotle's works belong to this category and their obscure passages should be left to the reader to judge. The same holds for books dealing with public or private matters of great importance and for the mysteries of the faith as contained in Holy Writ. In each of those cases the translator should never interpose his own judgment.

You must follow the original closely if you want to carry one of its characteristics across. That would be the way to translate Apuleius' *Golden Ass*; to highlight its remarkably comic style that is apt to make people laugh. If you cannot do that you will have to follow the inclination of your own nature which is likely to be your best guide, as long as you have been well educated. You should also struggle with your model if you are able to do so and make the work look better than it did when you received it by making it clearer in substance and easier to understand for those who read it. The original will look better when it is expressed in a more concise and advantageous manner, not when the translator is carried away by some sense of perverse vanity that encumbers correct, brilliant, and honest diction with rhetorical flourishes of all kinds, turning what is easy and rewarding into what is heavy and cumbersome. Why do translators debase the elegance and splendor of their original with words and figures of speech that are low, elaborate, and obscure? Out of a sense of overweening affectation that makes them display their eloquence without taking the nature and power of the text into account. They think they are about to produce a better style if they include words that are very rare, exotic, or old fashioned.

Jacques Pelletier du Mans, 1517–1582. French poet and grammarian.

Extract from his *Art Poétique* ("Poetics") published in 1555.

Translation is the truest kind of imitation. If you want to imitate you simply want to do as another does. The translator submits not only to the imagination of another but also to the way in which he orders his material and even to his elocution, as far as possible, and as far as the nature of the language he translates into allows, since a text very often owes its impact to a judicious choice of words and locutions. If that is lost the author loses all his elegance and the sense of what he says is betrayed. And yet translation means great labor more than great praise. If you render the original faithfully, to the best of your ability, you will only gain respect for having redrawn the original portrait, but fame remains with the original. If you render it badly all the blame falls on you. If your patron has not said things well you are considered a man of bad judgment for not having chosen a better model. In short a translator is never called an author. But do I want to discourage translators for all that? Certainly not, and still less do I want to deprive them of the praise that is their due since they are one of the reasons why France is, at least, able to begin to taste good things. They even derive a benefit from it all: if they translate well their author's name will make their own name live on. It is surely no small thing to have your own name written in good places. Those who write original works often run the risk of not living as long as translators, especially since a good translation is worth more than a bad original. What is more, well-made translations are able to greatly enrich a language. The translator can turn a beautiful Latin or Greek phrase into French and he can bring the weight of sentences, the majesty of clauses, and the elegance of the foreign language to his new country. These are two points that count in his favor since they come close to general concepts. The translator should be a little more wary when it comes to particulars, I think, just as he should be a little more wary with new words that are easy to spot and therefore suspect. A translator who has not presented any other work of his to the public, except translations, will not enjoy the favor of the readers when he coins new words, even though he is the one who must deal with new words all the time. That is the reason why the translator's task is not too highly thought of. Granted, when his author is excellent (and a prudent man will not translate any others) the translator will be allowed to use brand new words, as long as it is obvious that there are no other words available, and he will be praised for doing so. The continuous use of periphrasis, or circumlocutions, is too much of a drawback in translation. It also diminishes the merit of the author's ingenious work and, by the same token, the merit of translation as an art since these words belong to art and they might even be said to be so artificial that few people even know the laws that govern them. I can never stop wondering at those people who want to invoke Horace's authority to blame word for word translation.

Word for word translations do not find mercy in our eyes, not because they are against the law of translation but simply because two languages are never identical in their vocabulary. Ideas are common to the understanding of all men but words and manners of speech are particular to different nations. Do not enlist Cicero against me in this, because he does not praise the conscientious translator, and I will not praise him either. I mean the translator must keep the characteristics and the freshness of the language he translates into. I most decidedly maintain that he should not lose any part of the author's style or even choice of words when he deals with matters symbolized by two languages, for in that case the author's spirit and wit are often bound up with his style and choice of words. If anyone could translate the whole of Virgil into

French verse, phrase for phrase and word for word, he would deserve the highest praise. For how could a translator better do his duty than by coming as close as possible to the author he is subject to? Furthermore, think of the grandeur involved in having a second language convey all the elegance of the first while also keeping its own. But that is impossible, as I said before.

August Wilhelm Schlegel, 1767–1845. German critic, translator, and literary historian.

Extract from "Homers Werke von Johann Heinrich Voss" ("The Works of Homer by Johann Heinrich Voss"), published in 1796.

A language must completely take the place of another, so that those common elements that cannot be regulated by means of general prescriptions can be observed in addition to its rules. All poetic translation, which aims not just at meaning in general, but rather at the most intricate connotations, remains an imperfect approximation. No proof is needed that whatever license an original poet is allowed should also be allowed in full to a poet who translates, because he finds himself in a much less favorable situation. But it is just as certain that there are fixed limits for any language, whether caused by its original nature that endures for ever, or by evolution from time immemorial. You cannot go beyond those limits without incurring the justified reproach that you are not speaking a valid language that is recognized as such, but rather a jargon of your own invention. No necessity can be adduced as a justification for this.

The problem of the extent to which the individual has the right to contribute to the improvement of language has been much discussed of late. The history of languages proves that individual writers, especially poets, are able to exert an immeasurably large influence in this matter by means of their example. Much has, moreover, initially been condemned as corrupting a language, which later entered into that very language and proved itself to be rather an ennobling factor. Proposals to introduce into a language an element that is not yet available in it, should therefore not be rejected without thorough consideration. Like all human institutions, language, that marvelous charter of our higher destiny, also strives for the better, and the individual who becomes an organ of this general desire by engaging in certain endeavors, deserves well of language. There is only one indispensable condition: that he should not demolish while engaged in the act of construction. The innovation proposed should not be allowed to contradict what is already firmly established. If a language were merely something pieced together, made up of similar or dissimilar components, a formless mass, one would be allowed to change it or add to it at will, and every enrichment would be a gain, without exception. But language is an ordered whole, or at least it is meant to be gradually growing into one. All its elements attract or reject each other according to the laws of kinship and similarity. General forms pervade it, bring matter to life and bind it together with their power. The simpler its laws, the more encompassing and coherent, the more perfectly it will be organized. The more freedom establishes itself parallel to these laws, not in opposition to them, the more a language is adapted to poetic use. Excess of positive law-giving that leaves little or no maneuvering space for the development of original dispositions is a great evil, both in language and in the state. If what is being said about the much praised plasticity of our language holds true indeed, we do not suffer from this, at least not in comparison with other languages. We realize all the more easily that we are under the obligation no longer to impose anything on it that would be contrary to its nature, that could never melt into it until it became of the same nature. To be able to model oneself on a foreign nature, in the act of recreation, is true praise only when one has to assert one's independence at the same time and when one does, in fact, assert it.

The language-shaping artist's real domain begins, therefore, where the grammarian's judicial functions cease. There are only a few cases in which the latter is allowed to interfere with the former's business, namely when he tries to censure a use of language that is obviously wrong and whimsical, one that obtains only in certain locutions and runs counter to the general analogy. He always does so at his own risk. Every positive law of language is a matter of general consensus anyway (as is language itself), if not in its origin, then at least in its developed form, and only that same power that laid down the law is able to revoke it. The fact that one often fails to observe an inner necessity in this does not in the least detract from the status of language use. If you were to operate only with the principles of philosophical grammar, without any help from the individual, or even the whimsical, you could invent a kind of logical code notation, but never a living language. What has been irrevocably decided by consensus will prevail, even if you are able to show that chance did play a large part in the decision. You must also be aware of confusing chance events with characteristic idiosyncrasies. A law you might be inclined to think of as one of the tyrannical tricks of much maligned common usage if you observe it in isolation, often acquires a high degree of appropriateness, and even a kind of individual necessity that can be felt, rather than represented, when considered within the context of the components and the general structure of the language that promulgates that law.

Percy Bysshe Shelley, 1792–1822. English poet, thinker, and translator.

From "A Defence of Poetry," written in 1821, published in 1840.

Sounds as well as thoughts have relation both between each other and towards that which they represent, and a perception of the order of these relations has always been found connected with a perception of the order of the relations of thought. Hence the language of poets has ever affected a sort of uniform and harmonious recurrence of sound, without which it were not poetry, and which is scarcely less indispensable to the communication of its influence, than the words themselves without reference to that peculiar order. Hence the vanity of translation; it were as wise to cast a violet into a crucible that you might discover the formal principles of its colour and odour, as seek to transfuse from one language into another the creations of a poet. The plant must spring again from its seed or it will bear no flower – and this is the burthen and the curse of Babel.

Gaius Caecilius Plinius Secundus, 61/62–112/113. Roman writer and polymath.

Extract from the *Epistolae* ("Letters"), written between 97 and 109.

It is very beneficial to translate from Greek into Latin and from Latin into Greek, and people keep advising us to do so. This exercise provides you with a vocabulary both rich and apt, and with an abundance of stylistic figures and resources that can be used for further development. Moreover, the imitation of excellent models engenders an equally felicitous facility of invention.

Again, beautiful features of the text that may have escaped the reader's attention will not be missed by the translator. In this way you will acquire both taste and critical sense.

Johann Christoph Gottsched, 1700–1766. German literary theorist and translator.

Extract from the *Critische Dichtkunst* ("Critical Poetics") published in 1743.

Translation is precisely what the copying of a given model is to a beginner in the art of painting. We know that the works of great masters are copied with pleasure and diligence by mediocre artists or by beginners who would like to make their way. While they copy the design and the nuances and the full painting, they observe with great acumen every detail of the original artist's art and skill, the sum total of their example's beauty and perfection. They also make up a hundred little rules for themselves while they are working. They commit to memory a hundred technical tricks and advantages that are not immediately known to all and that they would have never discovered by themselves. Indeed, even their hand acquires a certain ability that guides the brush with more confidence. The same holds true for the translator.

Thomas Carlyle, 1795–1881. Scottish essayist, historian, and social thinker.

Extract from the essay "The State of German Literature," 1827.

Two centuries ago, translations from the German were comparatively frequent in England: Luther's *Table-Talk* is still a classic in our language; nay, Jacob Böhme has found a place among us, and this not as a dead letter, but as a living apostle to a still living sect of our religionists. In the next century, indeed, translation ceased; but then it was, in a great measure, because there was little worth translating.

Translators are of the same faithless and stolid race that they have ever been: the particle of gold they bring us over is hidden from all but the most patient eye, among shiploads of yellow sand and sulphur. Gentle Dulness, too, in this as in all other things, still loves her yoke. The Germans, though much more attended to, are perhaps not less mistaken than before.

The Germans study foreign nations in a spirit which deserves to be oftener imitated. It is their honest endeavour to understand each, with its own peculiarities, in its own special manner of existing; not that they may praise it, or censure it, or attempt to alter it, but simply that they may see its manner of existing as the nation itself sees it, and so participate in whatever worth or beauty it has brought into being. Of all literatures, therefore, the German has the best as well as the most translations.

Chapter 6

The technique of translating

Antoine Lemaistre lapses into the pedantic with his tenth rule of translation: "our prose pretends to have no rhymes, for as a general rule rhymes are avoided in prose." Attempts to regulate the production of translation with a view to insuring the production of the best possible translations have always smacked of the pedantic, the obvious, and the predictable. For every Erasmus who states: "I prefer to sin through excessive scrupulousness rather than through excessive license," there is a Chapman who counters: "always conceiving how pedantical and absurd it is in the interpretation of any author . . . to turn him word for word."

Rule-giving in translation is a thankless undertaking precisely because translation involves much more than the search for the best linguistic equivalent. In Matthew Arnold's words everybody would agree that "the translator's 'first duty is to be faithful,' but the question at issue between them is, in what faithfulness consists." That question cannot be answered on purely linguistic grounds.

It is therefore absurdly reductionist to define the goal of translation studies as the mere formulation of "rules" for translating. To do so is to deny not only the complexity of the phenomenon under discussion, but also the many ways in which a less reductionist approach to it can help shed light on central issues in the study of culture and acculturation.

Desiderius Erasmus, 1466–1536. Dutch humanist, philologist, social and religious thinker, and translator.

Extracts from the "Letter to William Warham," dated 1506.

To turn excellent Greek into excellent Latin you need an exceptional craftsman who has greatly enriched his knowledge of the two languages by accumulating an abundance of material. He must also possess a piercing eye that is always wakeful, and that is why for many centuries nobody in this field has been voted unanimously into this position.

I have scrupulously tried to produce a literal translation, forcing myself to keep the shape of the Greek poems, and also their style, as much as possible. My goal has been to transcribe verse for verse, almost word for word, and I have tried very hard to render the power and the weight of the phrase intelligible to Latin ears with the greatest fidelity, maybe because in translating the classics I do not completely approve of that freedom Cicero allows himself and others to excess I would say, or maybe because I prefer to sin through excessive scrupulousness rather than through excessive license since I am a novice in translation. I would rather be seen sinking into the sands of the shore than be shipwrecked in the middle of the waves. As I was going to make mistakes anyway I decided I would rather have men of letters deplore a lack of brilliance and ornamentation in my work than a lack of exactness. Finally, I did not wish to declare myself a paraphraser nor to prepare for myself all the refuges many others use to hide their ignorance, in which they avoid being caught by seeking protection behind their own darkness.

Antoine Lemaistre, 1608–1650. French religious writer and translator.

Extract from his *Règles de la traduction française* ("Rules of French Translation"), published in 1650.

1   The first point you must take into consideration when you translate into French is that you must be extremely literal and faithful, i.e. you must render into our language all that is in the Latin and you should do that so well that if Cicero had spoken our language he would have spoken as we make him speak in our translation.

2 You must try to render one felicitous passage by means of another and one figure of speech by means of another. You must try to imitate the author's style and to come as close to it as you can. You must vary the constructions and the figures of speech and make the translation into a painting, a vivid representation of what you translate, so that people will say that French is as beautiful as Latin and have the confidence to quote famous authors in French instead of in Latin.

3 We must distinguish between the purity of our verse and the beauty of our prose. The beauty of our verse is to be found in its rhymes, at least in part, whereas our prose claims to have no rhymes since rhymes are avoided in prose, as a general rule.

4 We must not write long sentences in our translations, nor affect a style that is too concise. Since our language runs longer than Latin anyway and needs more words to render the whole sense, we must try to strike a just balance between excessive abundance of words that would make the style sluggish, and excessive brevity that would make it obscure.

5 All parts of a sentence must be so well measured and so equal among themselves that they are perfectly symmetrical – as far as possible.

6 We must not put anything in our translation if we cannot justify it, or explain why we put it in. That is more difficult than you think.

7 We must be careful never to begin two sentences, and certainly not two parts of a sentence with a particle like "for, but," and the like.

8 We must also try never to use words with the same initial sounds in succession, as in "which one withholds," or "can conflict," since the whole point of harmony in discourse is that it should be pleasing to the ears, not the eyes.

9 The most beautiful part of a sentence is always the one that is below or above the halfway mark of a great heroic line, i.e. the part that consists of five or seven syllables.

10 When a sentence is too long or too complex in Latin or Greek it must be cut into a number of small parts in the translation.

George Chapman c.1559–1634. English poet, dramatist, and translator. His translation of Homer remained the standard English translation for two centuries.

Extracts from the prefatory texts to his translation of the *Iliad*, first published in 1598, republished in 1611.

Extract from "To the Reader"

Custom hath made even th'ablest agents err
    In these translations; all so much apply
Their poems and cunnings word for word to render
    Their patient authors, when they may as well
Make fish with fowl, camels with whales, engender,
    Or their tongues' speech in other mouths compell.
For, even as different a production
    Ask Greek and English, since they in sounds
And letters shun one form and unison;
    So have their sense and elegancy bounds
In their distinguish'd natures, and require
    Only a judgment to make both consent
In sense and elocution; and aspire,
    As well to reach the spirit that was spent
In his example, as with art to pierce
    His grammar, and etymology of words.

                so the brake
That those translators stick in, that affect
    Their word-for-word traductions (where they lose
The free grace of their natural dialect,
    And shame their authors with a forced gloss)
I laugh to see; and yet as much abhor
    More license from the words than may express
Their full compression, and make clear the author;
    From whose truth, if you think my feet digress,
Because I use needful paraphrases . . .
See that my conversion much abates
    The license they [previous translators] take, and
    more shows him too,
Whose right not all those great learn'd men have done,
    In some main parts, that were his commentors.

Extract from "The Preface to the Reader"

And much less I weigh the frontless detractions of some stupid ignorants, that, no more knowing me than their own beastly ends, and I ever (to my knowledge) blest from their sight, whisper behind me vilifyings of my translation, out of the French affirming them, when both in French, and all other languages but his own, our with-all-skill-enriched Poet is so poor and unpleasing that no man can discern from whence flowed his so generally given eminence, and admiration. And therefore (by any reasonable creature's conference of my slight comment and conversion) it will easily appear how I shun them, and whether the original be my rule or not. In which he shall easily see, I understand the understandings of all other interpreters and commentors in places of his most depth, importance, and rapture. In whose exposition and illustration, if I abhor from the sense that others wrest and wrack out of him, let my best detractor examine how the Greek word warrants me. For my other fresh fry, let them fry in their foolish galls, nothing so much weighed as the barkings of puppies, or foisting hounds, too vile to think of our sacred Homer, or set their profane feet within their lives' lengths of his thresholds. If I fail in something, let my full performance in other some restore me; haste spurring me on with other necessities.

To show my detractors that they have no reason to vilify my circumlocution sometimes, when their most approved Grecians, Homer's interpreters generally, hold him fit to be so converted. Yet how much I differ, and with what authority, let my impartial and judicial reader judge. Always conceiving how pedantical and absurd an affectation it is in the interpretation of any author (much more of Homer) to turn him word for word, when (according to Horace and other best lawyers to translators) it is the part of every knowing and judicial interpreter, not to follow the number and order of words, but the material things themselves, and sentences to weigh diligently, and to clothe and adorn them with words, and such a style and form of oration, as are most apt for the language in which they are converted. If I have not turned him in any place falsely (as all other his interpreters have in many, and most of his chief places) if I have not left behind me any of his sentences, elegancy, height, intention, and invention, if in some few places (especially in my first edition, being done so long since, and following the common tract) I be something paraphrastical and faulty, is it justice in that poor fault (if they will needs have it so) to drown all the rest of my labour?

Alexander Pope, 1688–1744. English poet, satirist, critic, and translator.

Extract from the preface to his translation of the *Iliad*, published in 1715.

Having now spoken of the Beauties and Defects of the Original, it remains to treat of the Translation, with the same view to the chief Characteristic. As far as that is seen in the main Parts of the Poem, such as the *Fable, Manners*, and *Sentiments*, no Translator can prejudice it but by willful Omissions or Contractions. As it also breaks out in every particular *Image, Description*, and *Simile*; whoever lessens or too much softens those, takes off from this chief Character. It is the first grand Duty of an Interpreter to give his Author entire and unmaim'd; and for the rest, the *Diction* and *Versification* only are his proper Province; since these must be his own, but the others he is to take as he finds them.

   It should then be consider'd what Methods may afford some Equivalent in our Language for the Grace of these in the Greek. It is certain no literal Translation can be just to an excellent Original in a superior Language: but it is a great Mistake to imagine (as many have done) that a rash Paraphrase can make amends for this general Defect; which is no less in danger to lose the Spirit of an Ancient, by deviating into the modern Manners of Expression. If there be sometimes a *Darkness*, there is often a *Light* in Antiquity, which nothing better preserves than a Version almost literal. I know no Liberties one ought to take, but those which are necessary for transfusing the Spirit of the Original, and Supporting the Poetical Style of the Translation: and I will venture to say, there have not been more Men misled in former times by a servile dull Adherence to the Letter, than have been deluded in ours by a chimerical insolent Hope of raising and improving their Author. It is not to be doubted that the *Fire* of the poem is what a Translator should principally regard, as it is most likely to expire in his managing: However it is his safest way to be content with preserving this to his utmost in the Whole, without endeavouring to be more than he finds his Author is, in any particular Place. 'Tis a great Secret in Writing to know when to be plain, and when poetical and figurative; and it is what *Homer* will teach us if we will but follow modestly in his Footsteps, where his Diction is bold and lofty, let us raise ours as high as we can; but where his is plain and humble, we ought not to be deterr'd from imitating him by the fear of incurring the Censure of a meer *English* Critick. Nothing that belongs to *Homer* seems to have been more commonly mistaken than the just Pitch of his Style: Some of his Translators having swell'd into Fustian in a proud Confidence of the *Sublime*; others sunk into Flatness, in a cold and timorous Notion of *Simplicity*. Methinks I see these different Followers of Homer, some seating and straining after him by violent Leaps and Bounds (the certain Signs of false Mettle), others slowly and servilely creeping in his Train, while the Poet himself is all the time proceeding with an unaffected and equal Majesty before them. However of the two Extreams one could sooner pardon Frenzy than Frigidity: No Author is to be envy'd for such Commendations as he may gain by that Character of Style which his Friends must agree together to call *Simplicity*, and the rest of the world will call *Dullness*. There is a *graceful* and *dignify'd* Simplicity, as well as a *bald* and *sordid* one, which differ as much from each other as the Air of a *plain* Man from that of a *Sloven*: 'Tis one thing to be tricked up, and another not to be dress'd at all. Simplicity is the Mean between Ostentation and Rusticity.

That which in my Opinion ought to be the Endeavour of any one who translates *Homer*, is above all things to keep alive that Spirit and Fire which makes his chief Character. In particular Places, where the Sense can bear any Doubt, to follow the strongest and most Poetical, as most agreeing with that Character. To copy him in all the Variations of his Style, and the different Modulations of his Numbers. To preserve in the more active if descriptive Parts, a Warmth and Elevation; in the more sedate or narrative, a Plainness and Solemnity; in the Speeches a Fullness and Perspicuity; in the Sentences a Shortness and Gravity. Not to neglect even the little Figures and Turns on the Words, nor sometimes the very Cast of the Periods. Neither to omit or confound any Rites or Customs of Antiquity. Perhaps too he ought to include the whole in a shorter Compass, than has hitherto been done by any Translator who has tolerably preserved either the Sense or Poetry. What I should farther recommend to him, is to study his Author rather from his own Text than from any Commentaries, how learned soever, or whatever Figure they make in the Estimation of the world. To consider him attentively in Comparison with *Virgil* above all the Ancients, and with *Milton* above all the Moderns. Next these the Archbishop of *Cambray*'s *Telemachus* may give him the truest Idea of the Spirit and Turn of our Author, and *Bossu's* admirable treatise of the Epic Poem the justest Notion of his Design and Conduct. But after all, with whatever Judgment and Study a Man may proceed, or with whatever Happiness he may perform such a Work; he must hope to please but a few, those only who have at once a Taste of Poetry, and competent Learning. For to satisfy such as want either, is not in the Nature of his Undertaking; since a meer Modern Wit can like nothing that is not *Modern*, and a Pedant nothing that is not *Greek*.

August Wilhelm Schlegel, 1767–1845. German critic, translator, and literary historian.

Extract from his "Schreiben an Herrn Reimer" ("Letter to Herrn Reimer") dated 1828.

In my opinion all annotations of individual passages should deal with objects, not words. Shakespeare is full of obscurities. Some of them are, if not intentional, at least original and in part characteristic; they arise from the compressed style, the bold liberties, the quick transitions from one metaphor to another. Other obscurities have come into being by chance, in the course of time. In these cases the translator may take a mild turn in the direction of clarity and become a kind of practical commentator, without weakening or paraphrasing the original.

What is the aim of poetic recreation? I think it should provide those who have no access to the original with as pure and uninterrupted an appreciation of it as possible. The translator should therefore not resuscitate in the notes the problems he has already solved in the text. What use does the natural friend of poetry have for the laboriousness of textual criticism, variants, conjectures, emendations? The few learned readers able to compare will see at once which edition the translator used.

So it would seem that we need explanations of objects only for the educated reader who is not a scholar, and we should put them either under the text, or with a reference at the end of the play. But who is going to check in Volume Three? A much more important need would be met by introductions of the kind I have attempted for *Romeo and Juliet*. In every one of Shakespeare's plays the reader is transported to a strange world, and he has to acclimatize to it first. Nothing can shed more light on the poet's profound wit and the creative power of his genius than a comparison between the new material of his works, be they true or apocryphal stories, novellas, fairy tales, legends, etc., and the end result achieved by the poetic alchemist himself.

In this case one should not try to save paper, in my opinion, but give whole passages from Holinshed in a literal translation, or in extracts, as an appendix to the historical plays. Sometimes the source is known, as in the Roman plays, but few readers will be so familiar with Plutarch that they would immediately think of the exact hints supplied by the biographer Shakespeare used and developed for his characterization. It would often be as interesting as it is instructive (in the case of *King Lear*, for instance) not to be satisfied with the nearest source but to go back to the most remote source available. And what is the most remote source of these apocryphal stories? Ask about and see if any readers will be able to answer that question. This type of research occupies a middle ground between textual criticism and the artistic evaluation of the work as a whole; it may, of course, be instrumental in preparing the way for the latter.

Dante Gabriel Rossetti, 1828–1882. English poet and painter.

Two extracts from *Dante and His Circle*, published in 1861.

A translation (involving as it does the necessity of settling many points without discussion) remains perhaps the most direct form of commentary.

The life-blood of rhythmical translation is this commandment: that a good poem shall not be turned into a bad one. The only true motive for putting poetry into a fresh language must be to endow a fresh nation, as far as possible, with one more possession of beauty. Poetry not being an exact science, literality of rendering is altogether secondary to this chief law. I say *literality*, – not fidelity, which is by no means the same thing. When literality can be combined with what is thus the primary condition of success, the translator is fortunate, and must strive his utmost to unite them; when such an object can only be attained by paraphrase, that is his only path.

The task of the translator (and with all humility be it spoken) is one of some self-denial. Often would he avail himself of any special grace of his own idiom and epoch, if only his will belonged to him; often would some cadence serve him but for his author's structure – some structure but for his author's cadence: often the beautiful turn of a stanza must be weakened to adopt some rhyme which will tally, and he sees the poet revelling in abundance of language where himself is scantily supplied. Now he would slight the matter for the music, and now the music for the matter; but no, he must deal to each alike. Sometimes too a flaw in the work galls him, and he would fain remove it, doing for the poet that which his age denied him; but no, – it is not in the bond. His path is like that of Aladdin through the enchanted vault: many are the precious fruits and flowers which he must pass by unheeded in search for the lamp alone; happy if at last, when brought to light, it does not prove that his old lamp has been exchanged for a new one, glittering indeed to the eye, but scarcely of the same virtue nor with the same genius as it summons.

Matthew Arnold, 1822–1888. English poet, critic, educator, and translator.

Extract from "On Translating Homer," published in 1861.

It is disputed what aim a translator should propose to himself in dealing with his original. Even this preliminary is not yet settled. On one side it is said that the translation ought to be such "that the reader should, if possible, forget that it is a translation at all, and be lulled into the illusion that he is reading an original work – something original (if the translation be in English) from an English hand." The real original is in this case, it is said, "taken as a basis on which to rear a poem that shall affect our countrymen as the original may be conceived to have affected its natural hearers." On the other hand, Mr. Newman, who states the forego-ing doctrine only to condemn it, declares that he "aims at precisely the opposite: to retain every peculiarity of the original, so far as he is able, *with the greater care the more foreign it may happen to be*; so that it may never be forgotten that he is imitating, and imitating in a different material." The translator's "first duty," says Mr. New-man, "is a historical one, to be *faithful*." Probably both sides would agree that the translator's "first duty is to be faithful;" but the question at issue between them is, in what faithfulness consists.

My one object is to give practical advice to a translator; and I shall not the least concern myself with theories of translation as such. But I advise the translator not to try "to rear on the basis of the *Iliad*, a poem that shall affect our countrymen as the original may be conceived to have affected its natural hearers;" and for this simple reason, that we cannot possibly tell *how* the *Iliad* "affected its natural hearers." It is probably meant merely that he should try to affect Englishmen powerfully, as Homer affected Greeks powerfully; but this direction is not enough, and can give no real guidance. For all great poets affect their hearers powerfully, but the effect of one poet is one thing, that of another poet another thing: it is our translator's business to reproduce the effect of Homer, and the most powerful emotion of the unlearned English reader can never assure him whether he has reproduced this, or whether he has produced something else. So, again, he may follow Mr. Newman's directions, he may "retain every peculiarity of his original," but who is to assure him, who is to assure Mr. Newman himself, that, when he has done this, he has done that for which Mr. Newman enjoins this to be done, "adhered closely to Homer's manner and habit of thought?" Evidently the translator needs some more practical directions than these. No one can tell him how Homer affected the Greeks; but there are those who can tell him how Homer affects *them*. These are scholars; who possess, at the same time with knowledge of Greek, adequate poetical taste and feeling. No translation will seem to them of much worth compared with the original; but they alone can say whether the translation produces more or less the same effect upon them as the original. They are the only competent tribunal in the matter: the Greeks are dead; the unlearned Englishman has not the data for judging; and no man can safely confide in his own single judgment of his own work. Let not the translator, then, trust to his notions of what the ancient Greeks would have thought of him; he will lose himself in the vague. Let him not trust to what the ordinary English reader thinks of him; he will be taking the blind for his guide. Let him not trust to his own judgment of his own work; he may be misled by individual caprices. Let him ask how his work affects those who both know Greek and can appreciate poetry.

Chapter 7

Central texts and central cultures

The translators of the *Authorized Version* warn in their preface that "he that meddleth with men's religion in any part, meddleth with their custom, nay, with their freehold." If a text is considered to embody the core values of a culture, if it functions as that culture's central text, translations of it will be scrutinized with the greatest of care, since "unacceptable" translations may well be seen to subvert the very basis of the culture itself. This is what Sir Thomas More accuses Tyndale of when he makes the charge that "Tyndale changed in his translation the common known words to the intent to make a change in the faith." If, on the other hand, a certain culture considers itself "central" with regard to other cultures, it is likely to treat the texts produced by those cultures in the rather cavalier manner Herder deplores in the French translations of Homer: "Homer must enter France a captive and dress according to their fashion, so as not to offend their eyes." Edward Fitzgerald, a member of the central culture that succeeded in France, actually boasts: "It is an amusement for me to take what liberties I like with these Persians."

It is in the treatment of texts that play a central role within a culture and in the way a central culture translates texts produced by cultures it considers peripheral, that the importance of such factors as ideology, poetics, and the Universe of Discourse is most obviously revealed.

Sir Thomas More, 1477–1535 English humanist, writer, and statesman.

Extract from the conclusion of the second book of the *Confutation of Tyndale's Answer*, 1532.

For every man well knoweth that the intent and purpose of my dialogue was none other, but to make the people perceive that Tyndale changed in his translation the common known words to the intent to make a change in the faith. As for example that he changed the word church into this word congregation, because he would bring it in question which were the church and set forth Luther's heresy that the church which we should believe and obey, is not the common known body of all Christian realms remaining in the faith of Christ . . . but that the church which we should believe and obey, were some secret unknown sort of evil living and worse believing heretics. And that he changed priest into senior because he intended to set forth Luther's heresy teaching that priesthood is no sacrament but the office of a lay man or a lay woman appointed by the people to preach. And that he changed penance into repenting because he would set forth Luther's heresy teaching that penance is no sacrament.

And I made my book to good Christian people that know such heresies for heresies to give them warning that by scripture of his own false forging (for so is his false translation, and not the scripture of god) he should not beguile them, and make them ween the thing were otherwise than it is in deed. For as for such as are so mad all ready, to take those heresies for other than heresies, and are thereby them selves no faithful folk but heretics, if they list not to learn and leave off, but longer to lie still in their false belief: it were all in vain to give them warning thereof. For when their wills be bent thereto, and their hearts set thereon: there will no warning serve them. And therefore sith Tyndale hath here confessed in his defense that he made such changes for the setting forth of such things as I said: it is enough for good Christian men that know these things for heresies, to abhor and burn up his books.

And yet defending him self so fondly, and teaching open heresies so shamefully: he sayeth it appeareth that there was no cause to burn his translation, wherein such changes be found as ye see, and being changed for such causes as him self confesseth that is to wit for a foundation of such pestilent heresies as him self

affirmeth and writeth in his abominable books: he might much
better if he cut a man's throat in the open street, say there were no
cause to hang him but bid men seek up his knife and see it him
safe. This might he in good faith much better say then, than he
may now say that there is no cause to burn his translation. With
the falsehood whereof and his false heresies brought in there
withal: he hath killed and destroyed diverse men, and may
hereafter many, some in body, some in soul, and some in both
twain.

Anonymous

Extract from "The Translators to the Reader," the
translators' preface to the 1611 *Authorized Version* of the
Bible.

For he that meddleth with men's religion in any part, meddleth
with their custom, nay, with their freehold; and though they find
no content in that which they have, yet they cannot abide to hear
of altering.

Translation it is that openeth the window, to let in the light;
that breaketh the shell, that we may eat the kernel; that putteth
aside the curtain, that we may look into the most holy place; that
removeth the cover of the well, that we may come by the water,
even as Jacob rolled away the stone from the mouth of the well, by
which means the flocks of Laban were watered. Indeed without
translation into the vulgar tongue, the unlearned are but like
children at Jacob's well (which was deep) without a bucket or
something to draw with.

Therefore blessed be they, and most honoured be their name,
that break the ice, and giveth onset upon that which helpeth
forward to the saving of souls . . . Yet for all that, as nothing is
begun and perfected at the same time, and the latter thoughts are
thought to be the wiser: so, if we building upon their foundation
that went before us, and being holpen by their labours, do
endeavour to make better what they left so good; no man, we are
sure, hath cause to mislike us; they, we persuade ourselves, if they
were alive, would thank us.

And what can the King command to be done, that will bring
him more true honour than this? and wherein could they that
have been set at work, approve their duty to the King, yea their
obedience to God, and love his Saints more, than by yielding their
service, and all that is within them, for the furnishing of the work?

A man may be counted a virtuous man, though he have made many slips in his life (else there were none virtuous, for *in many things we offend all*) also a comely man and lovely, though he have some warts upon his hand; yea not only freckles upon his face, but also scars. No cause therefore why the word translated should be denied to be the word, or forbidden to be current, notwithstanding that some imperfections and blemishes may be noted in the setting forth of it.

We must answer a third cavill and objection of theirs against us, for altering and amending our translations so oft; wherein truly they deal hardly and strangely with us. For to whom ever was it imputed for a fault (by such as were wise) to go over that which he had done, and to amend it where he saw cause? . . . If we will be sons of the truth, we must consider what it speaketh, and trample upon our own credit, yea, and upon other men's too, if either be any hindrance to it.

To make a good one better, or out of many good ones, one principal good one, not justly to be excepted against; that hath been our endeavour, that our mark.

And in what sort did [the translators] assemble? In the trust of their own knowledge, or of their sharpness of wit, or deepness of judgement, as it were in an arm of flesh? At no hand. They trusted in him that hath the key of David, opening and no man shutting; they prayed to the Lord, the Father of our Lord . . . In this confidence, and with this devotion, did they assemble together, not too many, lest one should trouble another; and yet many, lest many things haply might escape them.

Therefore, as St. Augustine saith, that variety of translations is profitable for the finding out the sense of the Scriptures: so diversity of signification and sense in the margin, where the text is not so clear, must needs do good; yea, is necessary, as we are persuaded . . . They that are wise had rather have their judgements at liberty in differences of readings, than be captivated to one, when it may be the other.

We cannot follow a better pattern of elocution than God himself; therefore he using divers words, in his holy writ, and indifferently for one thing in nature: we, if we will not be superstitious, may use the same liberty in our English versions out of Hebrew and Greek, for that copy or store that he hath given us.

Johann Gottfried Herder, 1744–1803. German writer, philosopher, and translator.

Extracts from the *Fragmente* ("Fragments"), published in 1766 and 1767.

The real translator should therefore adapt words, manners of speaking, and combinations from a more developed language to his mother tongue, preferably from Greek and Latin but also from younger languages. Like older nations and their works, all older languages have more characteristic features than the languages that are not as old. Our language should therefore be able to learn more from them than from languages with which it claims close kinship.

The book is made: for the translator it is his bread and butter; for the publisher an article to sell in the market place; for the buyer a book in his library. And for literature? Nothing! Or even a negative contribution. Zero or less than zero.

The French, who are much too proud of their own taste, adapt all things to it, rather than try to adapt themselves to the taste of another time. Homer must enter France a captive and dress according to their fashion, so as not to offend their eyes. He has let them take his venerable beard and his old simple clothes away from him. He has to conform to French customs, and where his peasant coarseness still shows he is treated as a barbarian. But we poor Germans, who are still almost an audience without a fatherland, who are still without tyrants to dictate our taste, want to see him the way he is.

And the best translation cannot achieve this for Homer without the help of notes and explanations written in the highest critical spirit.

Johann Wolfgang von Goethe, 1749–1832. German poet, dramatist, novelist, and critic.

Extract from *Dichtung und Wahrheit* ("Poetry and Truth"), written between 1811 and 1814.

Wieland's translation of Shakespeare appeared. It was devoured, passed around, and recommended to friends and acquaintances. We Germans had the advantage that many important works of foreign nations were first translated in a light and bantering vein. The translations of Shakespeare into prose, first Wieland's, then Eschenburg's, were able to spread quickly as reading matter. They were generally intelligible and suited to the common reader. I respect both rhythm and rhyme because they are what makes poetry into poetry indeed. Yet what is left of a poet when he has been translated into prose is what is really deeply and thoroughly operative, what really shapes and improves. What remains is the pure, perfect essence. A blinding exterior often succeeds in deluding us into believing that such an essence is there when it is not, or in hiding it when it is. That is why I think translations into prose are more useful than translations into verse in the first stages of education. Boys, who turn everything into a joke, make fun of the sound of words and the fall of syllables, and destroy the deep essence of the noblest work out of a certain sense of parodistic devilry. I would therefore like you to consider whether we could not use a prose translation of Homer at this moment, provided it is worthy of the level German literature has reached by now. I leave this and my other remarks to the consideration of our worthy pedagogues who can rely on extensive experience in this matter. I simply want to remind you of Luther's Bible translation as an argument in favor of my proposal. Religion has benefited more from the fact that this excellent man translated a work written in the most different array of styles into a work all of one piece in our mother tongue, than it would have if he had aspired to recreate the original's idiosyncrasies down to the smallest detail. Luther also gave us the poetic, historical, imperative, and didactic tone we find in the Bible. And that, too, he gave us in one piece, so to speak. Later translators have tried in vain to make us enjoy the Book of Job, the Psalms, and other canticles in their poetic form. If you want to influence the masses a simple translation is always best. Critical translations vying with the original really are of use only for conversations the learned conduct among themselves.

Extract from the *West-Östlicher Diwan* ("Book of West and East"), published in 1819.

There are three kinds of translation. The first acquaints us with foreign countries on our own terms. A simple prosaic translation is the best in this respect. Since prose totally cancels all peculiarities of any kind of poetic art and since prose itself pulls poetic enthusiasm down to a kind of common water-level, it performs the greatest service in the beginning by surprising us with foreign excellence in the midst of our national homeliness, our everyday existence. It offers us a higher mood and real edification, and all the while we do not realize what is happening to us. Luther's Bible translation is sure to produce this kind of effect at any time.

Much would have been gained if the *Nibelungen* had been put into decent prose at the outset, and if it had been stamped a popular romance. Its singular, dark, noble, awesome sense of chivalry would then have addressed itself to us with its full strength. Those who have applied themselves more thoroughly to these matters of great antiquity will be best able to judge whether such a course of action is still advisable, or even feasible at the present moment.

A second epoch follows in which the translator really only tries to appropriate foreign content and reproduce it in his own sense, even though he tries to transport himself into foreign situations. I would like to call this kind of epoch the parodistic one, in the fullest sense of the word. Men of wit feel called to this kind of trade in most cases. The French use this method in their translations of all kinds of poetic works. Hundreds of examples can be found in the translations produced by Delille. Just as the French adapt foreign words to their own pronunciation, so do they treat feelings, thoughts, and even objects. For every foreign fruit they demand a counterfeit grown in their own soil.

Wieland's translations belong to this category. He, too, had a singular sense of taste and understanding that brought him close to antiquity and foreign countries only as far as he could still feel at ease. This excellent man may be considered the representative of his time. He has had an extraordinary impact, precisely because what he found pleasing, how he appropriated it, and how he communicated it in his turn, seemed pleasing and enjoyable to his contemporaries as well.

Since it is impossible to linger too long in either perfection or imperfection, and since one change must of necessity follow another, we have lived through the third epoch, which could be called the highest and final one, namely the one in which the aim is to make the original identical with the translation, so that one should be valued not instead of the other, but in the other's stead.

Originally this kind of translation had to overcome the greatest resistance, since the translator who attaches himself closely to his original more or less abandons the originality of his own nation, with the result that a third essence comes into existence, and the taste of the multitude must first be shaped to accept it.

Voss, who can never be praised enough, could not satisfy the public when he began to translate, but that same public slowly became receptive to his new manner and grew comfortable with it. Whoever is now able to see what happened, what versatility has come to the Germans, what rhetorical, rhythmical, metrical advantages are at the disposal of the talented and knowledgeable youngster, how Ariosto and Tasso, Shakespeare and Calderon are now presented to us twice and three times over as foreigners who have been made German, should hope that literary history will plainly state who was the first to take this road despite so many obstacles.

The works of von Hammer point for the most part to a similar treatment of Oriental masterpieces, in which approximation to the external form of the original is to be most recommended. The passages of a translation of Firdausi our friend has provided us with are unquestionably more useful when compared to those of an adaptor. In my opinion, adapting a poet is the saddest mistake a diligent translator, who is also well-suited to his task, could make. Yet since these three epochs are repeated and inverted in every literature, and since they can be in effect applied simultaneously, a translation into prose of the *Shah-nama* and the works of Nizami is still in order. It could be used for a quick reading that would serve to unlock the main sense. We would be pleased with the historical, the legendary, and the generally ethical, and we would move closer and closer to ways of thinking and feeling until we could totally fraternize with them at last.

Remember how we Germans awarded the most resolute recognition to such a translation of the *Sakuntala*. We can ascribe its great impact to the general prose in which the poem has been diluted. Yet the time has come for someone to offer it to us in a translation of the third type, which would do justice to the different dialects and to the rhythmical, metrical, and prosaic manners of speech in the original. Such a translation would allow us to enjoy the poem again with all its idiosyncrasies and would naturalize it for us.

Extract from *Schriften zur Literatur* ("Writings on Literature"), published in 1824.

There are two maxims in translation: one requires that the author of a foreign nation be brought across to us in such a way that we can look on him as ours. The other requires that we ourselves should cross over into what is foreign and adapt ourselves to its conditions, its peculiarities, and its use of language. There are enough perfect examples of both kinds, and educated people are familiar with the advantages of both. Our friend [Wieland], who wanted to find the middle way in this matter also, tried to reconcile both. But since he was a man of feeling he preferred the first maxim when in doubt.

August Wilhelm Schlegel, 1767–1845. German critic, translator, and literary historian.

Extract from "Wettstreit der Sprachen" ("Argument Between Languages"), published in 1798.

Frenchman:	Languages would be classified according to their ability to translate. I must protest against this in the name of my own language. The criterion is narrowly national in nature because the Germans translate every literary Tom, Dick, and Harry. We either do not translate at all, or else we translate according to our own taste.
German:	Which is to say, you paraphrase and you disguise.
Frenchman:	We look on a foreign author as a stranger in our midst. He has to dress according to our customs, and behave accordingly, if he aims to please.
German:	How narrow-minded of you to be pleased only by what is native.
Frenchman:	Such is our nature and education. Did the Greeks not Hellenize all things too?
German:	In your case it goes back to a narrow-minded nature and a conventional education. In our case education is our nature.

Extract from *Geschichte der klassischen Literatur* ("History of Classical Literature"), published in 1803.

Poetic translation is a very difficult art. One could write a lengthy essay on its principles, but not without devoting much attention to both grammatical and philological detail. Allow me to make just a few observations about it here, namely that this art was invented only a few years ago, if you leave a few exceptions out of consideration, and that its invention was reserved for German fidelity and perseverance. In the first period of their history, when they modelled their language after Greek forms, and not without violence, the Romans seem to have had relatively faithful translations of Greek poems, as far as we can judge from a few fragments, even though the translations were not altogether without rough and clumsy passages. In fact, everything started with translation in their case. Later, in what is called the Golden Age of their poetry, when it had evolved its own system of diction, it seems to have lost this ability more and more, and if people were not satisfied with free imitations, as is most often the case, the translations certainly lost character and became more mannered. Greek and Latin are, moreover, closely related; one could almost think of them as dialect and standard language, and in that case poetic recreation has been known to succeed to a very high degree, and without much of an effort, as in the case of Spanish and Italian, for instance. Other nations, however, have adopted a totally conventional phraseology in poetry and made it into an unbreakable rule, so that it is totally impossible to make a poetic translation of anything whatsoever into their language – French is an example and so is contemporary English, albeit to a lesser extent.

It is as if they want every foreigner among them to dress and behave according to the customs of the nation, and that explains why they never really get to know a foreigner. If they torture themselves to achieve the highest possible fidelity, they do so in prose, which totally changes everything: they offer us the dead parts, the living breath has gone. Literalness is a long way from fidelity. Fidelity means that the same or similar impressions are produced, for these are the heart of the matter. That is why all translations of verse into prose should be proscribed, because meter should not just be an external ornament (just as it is not, in real poems); rather it ranks among the original and essential prerequisites of poetry. Furthermore, since all metrical forms have a definite meaning, and their necessary character in a given language may very well be demonstrated (for unity of form and essence is the goal of all art, and the more they interpenetrate and reflect each other, the higher the perfection achieved), one of the first principles of the art of translation is that a poem should be recreated in the same meter, as far as the nature of the language allows. Translators are very much inclined to deviate from this, partly because it is very difficult and partly because they have grown fond of the practice as it has been accepted up to now: two very good reasons to proclaim the greatest stringency as a general law.

Edward Fitzgerald, 1809–1883. English translator and poet.

Extract from a letter written to E. B. Cowell in 1857.

It is an amusement for me to take what liberties I like with these Persians, who (as I think) are not Poets enough to frighten one from such excursions, and who really do want a little Art to shape them.

Chapter 8

Longer statements

The longer statements collected in the final part of this reader further discuss the main aspects of both the production and reception of translations highlighted in the preceding shorter extracts. Not all longer statements deal with all of these aspects, but they exhibit a remarkable continuity of thinking about the translation of literature within the tradition outlined here.

It has been one of the purposes of this reader to reveal the basic categories that can be seen to have been the foundation of much thinking about the translation of literature within that tradition. It will be clear that future studies of the phenomenon of literary translation run the risk of not being very productive if they tend to focus on, say, the technique of translation to the exclusion of the other categories mentioned. It should also be clear that a productive study of the translation of literature can, for the most part, be only socio-historical in nature. The most important consideration is not how words are matched on the page, but why they are matched that way, what social, literary, ideological considerations led translators to translate as they did, what they hoped to achieve by translating as they did, whether they can be said to have achieved their goals or not, and why.

Leonardo Bruni, called Aretino, 1374–1444. Italian humanist, translator of Plato and Aristotle.

Extracts from *De interpretatione recta* ("The Right Way to Translate") published in 1420.

When I translated Aristotle's *Nicomachean Ethics* from Greek into Latin, I added an introduction in which I discussed many of the mistakes made by previous translators and how I had corrected them. I hear that many people thought that my corrections were too harsh. Their argument runs as follows: even if the translators made mistakes they wrote down what they understood in good faith and for that they deserve praise, not blame. It would therefore be more fitting for moderate critics, their argument runs on, not to point out obvious mistakes but to produce a better translation, rather than to cut up their predecessors with words. I confess I have been a little too radical with my reprimands, but that radicalism originated in heartfelt indignation. I was distressed indeed at the sight of those books that are full of sweetness, elegance, and inestimable value in Greek, and I myself was pained to see how these books had turned out so vile and degraded in Latin because the translations are riddled with impurities. If I had found great joy in a most decorative and pleasing painting by Protogenes, Apelles, or Aglaophon, I would be upset if somebody should vilify that painting and I would raise both my voice and my hand against him. And so, when I saw how those books by Aristotle, which are far more brilliant and finely crafted than any painting, were degraded, I felt as if my soul had been crucified and I was greatly moved. If some people think I may have gone too far they should know that I was moved by a cause, such a worthy cause indeed that I might deserve a pardon if I did go too far. Yet in my own opinion I did not go too far, not even a little. Rather, my anger has saved both good taste and mankind. Think of that for a moment. Did I say anything against other translators' morals? Or against the way they live? Did I call them traitors, drunks, or lechers? Certainly not. Then what did I attack in them? Only their lack of experience in writing. And is that such a heavy insult, by God Almighty? And can a man not be a good man and still be either completely ignorant of all that pertains to writing, or not have the extensive experience I require of him? I do not call such a person a bad man, but merely a bad translator. I would say similar things about Plato if he wanted to steer a ship without knowing how. I would not detract from his philosophy in any way but I would simply say that he was inexperienced and inept as a captain.

I say that the full power of a translation resides in the fact that what is written in one language should be well translated into another. Nobody can do that well unless he has an experience of both languages that is both wide and deep. But that is not enough, since many people are eminently capable of understanding, though not of explaining, just as many people are able to judge a painting correctly even if they themselves do not paint, or just as many people are able to understand music without being able to sing.

A correct translation is therefore a great and difficult thing. First, of course, you need to know the language you are translating from, and that knowledge should not be limited or trivial, but great and supported by an experience that is deep and accurate, and steeped in the daily reading of philosophers, orators, poets, and all other writers. Unless you have read them all, grown with them, turned them over in your mind, and kept them there, you cannot understand the power and the meaning of the words, especially since Aristotle himself and also Plato were masters of literature, if I may say so, and made use of the most elegant modes in which the old poets, orators, and historians used to write, as well as of their more felicitous choice of words and turns of phrase. In their works, therefore, metaphors and figures of speech appear that mean one thing on the literal level and another on the level of traditional understanding.

The translator should therefore begin by ensuring that he knows the language he is going to translate from as well as is humanly possible, and he will never acquire that knowledge without a repeated, varied, and accurate reading of all kinds of writers. Furthermore, he should also know the language he translates into in such a way that he is able to dominate it and to hold it entirely in his power. If he has to render a word by another, therefore, he should not go begging for one, nor should he resort to loan-translation or leave the word in Greek because he does not know Latin. He should also be aware of the power and nature of words in all their subtle ramifications. Moreover, he should not be ignorant of figures of speech, nor of the way the best writers use the language. He should imitate them in his own writing and he should avoid novelty in word and figure of speech, especially if such a novelty is inept or barbaric.

All the elements mentioned above are necessary. In addition to them the translator should also have a good ear, so as not to weaken what has been said in an elegant or harmonious way, or to throw it off balance. Since all good writers, and most obviously Plato and Aristotle in their books, combine what they want to say about things with the art of writing itself, a translator worthy of that name must serve both masters. Translators are therefore likely to make the following mistakes: they will translate what has been aptly put and skillfully arranged by the author in such a way that it becomes inept, incoherent, and weak. Whoever is not so well educated in both style and substance that he is able to avoid all of these mistakes deserves to be censured and criticized when he takes up translating because he will either lead people into various mistakes by providing them with the wrong translation, or he will diminish his author's stature by making him seem ridiculous and absurd. And yet they will say that the man who publishes what he knows deserves praise, not blame, even if he is by no means well versed in those arts which require experience. A poet who writes bad lines does not deserve praise, even if he tried to write good ones. Rather we criticize him and reprimand him for trying to do what he knows not how. We also criticize a sculptor who makes a bad statue even if he did not do so on purpose, but just because he did not know any better. Those who learn to paint by trying to copy an existing painting ponder the problem of how to transfer the shape, the stance, the gait, and the contours of the body not as they would make them, but as somebody else did make them. The same process occurs in translation: the translator transforms himself into the original author with all his mind, will, and soul, and he also ponders the problem of how to transform the shape, the stance, the gait, the style, and all the other features, and how to express them. The result will be a wonderful translation.

Individual writers have their very own figures of speech. Cicero excels in abundance and number of words, Sallust in brevity and slenderness of style, Livy in sometimes all too stringent grandeur. In translating specific writers the good translator will conform to them in such a way that he renders their own figures of speech. If he translates from Cicero he will have to guide that author's great, expressive, and sonorous periods to their fullest circumference with the same abundance and variety. Sometimes he will have to make them flow faster and sometimes he will have to pull them together. If he translates from Sallust, on the other hand, he will have to sit in judgment on each of that author's few words and he will have to follow propriety and decorum first and foremost. To do so he will sometimes have to tighten the language and make it even more concise. If he translates from Livy he will have no choice but to imitate that author's figures of speech, since the translator is forcibly drawn into the style of the author he translates, and he will not find it easy to serve the sense except if he insinuates himself and modifies his author's phrasing and display of writing with the proper words and rhetorical figures. For this is the highest rule of translation: that the shape of the original text should be kept as closely as possible, so that understanding does not lose the words any more than the words themselves lose brilliance and craftsmanship.

But even if all good translation is difficult because of the many and varied features it is required to possess, the most difficult task of all is to translate effectively what the original author wrote in a copious and ornate style. The translator should be fully aware that it is necessary to intervene with full stops, commas, and periods in a text written in a copious style, to render the style clear and make comprehension possible. The translator should display the greatest zeal in trying to preserve the original's ornate diction and other features. If the translator fails to accomplish all this he will weaken his author's stature and diminish it. But he cannot possibly achieve it without expending much labor and acquiring much experience in matters of writing. The translator has to understand the particular features of each text, so to speak, and to render them in a similar way in the language he translates into. If the original displays two kinds of ornaments, one concerned with the words, the other with the content, both will represent difficulties for the translator, but the words more so than the content, primarily because ornaments of this kind often submit to a certain scansion, so that like should be rendered by like, or opposite by opposite, or contraries by contraries, which the Greeks call antitheta. Yet it often happens that Latin words consist of more syllables than their Greek counterparts, and just as often they do not easily correspond with sounds the ear is able to pick up. Interjections, which the orator throws in from time to time, tend to have a greater impact if they scan right, since slack and mutilated or inept cadences do not pierce in as effective a manner. The translator must learn all these things as best he can and use them to shape the mold of his scansion. And what am I to say about the ornaments of content that decorate the text in many ways and make it admirable, especially in the case of those superior ornaments used by the best writers? Could a translator possibly ignore these, pass them by, or translate them without preserving their stature, and go uncensored?

Petrus Danielus Huetius, 1630–1721. French bishop and educator.

Long extracts from "De optimo genere interpretandi" ("On the Best Way of Translating"), Book One of *De interpretatione libri duo* ("Two Books on Translation"), published in 1683. The work, written in the form of a dialogue, is often referred to, but almost never quoted from. This is its first partial translation into English.

THUANUS: First of all, it is obvious what interpretation is and how it is generally understood: an interpretation is *any text which makes more understandable what is hardly understood.* This holds true not only for translation from one language into another, but also for commentary, explanations of words, notes, paraphrases, metaphrases (whether they move closer to the original or stay farther away from it), and the like. The term can also be stretched to include the clarification of recondite disciplines, the elucidation of dreams and oracles, the solution of implicit problems and, finally, the elucidation of all that is unknown. For our purposes the term will be used in a stricter sense and taken to mean *the translation of a text from one language into another.* Translations can be made for two reasons. One is to learn languages and to improve your style. This is what pupils do in school when they translate from their mother tongue into Latin or from Latin into Greek, to prove to those who know these languages that they have understood the text, at least in part. The other reason is to explain a text to those who do not understand it. This state of affairs gives rise to two kinds of translation. We shall not deal with the first kind at this time and it will therefore be left out of this text. We shall define the second kind as follows: *a text written in a well-known language which refers to, and represents a text in a language which is not as well known.*

We shall be using this definition for the kind of interpretation we shall be dealing with throughout our text. This kind of interpretation can also be said to consist of two types. In the first type the translator does not respect his author all that much, nor the meaning underlying the words the author uses. He therefore writes either to instruct or amuse the reader, or to indulge his own creativity. In the other kind of translation the translator uses all his zeal and all his skill to render his author's writings as accurately as possible. The texts the older Roman poets translated from Greek into Latin verse can be seen to belong to the first kind. We must also list the condensed version here, in which a translator compresses a wordy author into some narrower compass in another language. And this, too, is the place to include paraphrase. Its definition comes to us from Quintilian, where he says: "I do not want a translation to be a paraphrase, but rather a struggle with and emulation of the original which renders the same sense." Periphrases and metaphrases also belong here since they translate texts more or less as the occasion arises, adding certain features, taking away others, and putting the text together again in a different shape. I would define a periphrase as that which explains by means of a greater number of words what can be said in one word, or in a few words. Moreover, Quintilian's description should not just be applied to what is explained in the same language, but also to what is explained in another.

The authors of this kind of translation set out to follow or imitate the authors of their originals, not to translate them, and a debate on the merits and demerits of this kind of translation does not fall within the scope of this text. We shall be dealing with the second type of translation here, and we shall try to establish how an author should be translated with the greatest fidelity and diligence. My translations of Polybius belong to this type, as do your translations of Chrysostomus, my dear Fronto. The work we now see being done more generally by contemporary translators also tends to fit in with this type. I think we have already shown sufficiently what the different types of texts are. What we must do now is to select the best kind from the type we shall be dealing with from now on, and to formulate its general principles.

I call that translation the best in which the author stays the closest possible first to his author's meaning, then, if both languages allow it, to his author's words and, finally, to his author's personal style. The translator should also take care not to diminish his author by omitting something, or to add to him by supplementing the text. Rather, he should show him whole, and show the best possible likeness in every part. In that way the translator will be seen to be nothing else than the expression of the author's image and likeness. The best possible likeness is that which renders the lines of the mouth, the color, the eyes, the shape of the face, and the way in which the body moves in such a manner that the absent man who is portrayed can be thought of as present. But a bad likeness pictures a thing in a manner different from what it is, more beautiful and with a happier countenance. We do not like translations that eat up the author's fat or put more fat on him, nor do we like translations that clear up obscure passages, correct mistakes, or sort out bad syntax. We would rather have a translation that shows us the whole author, closely copied in our native style, and one that makes it possible for us to either praise his virtues, should they be deserving of praise, or scoff at his vices. For who, except a young girl who loves herself too much and wants to please herself too much would praise a mirror that so disfigures the face that it reflects a rosy forehead, or a forehead full of vigor, or even a forehead tempered with decent splendor when shown a face of ghastly pallor, or a face that is shrivelled and emaciated, or even a face that shines with too much red color. Who would not mock a woman made up in such a way that she displays an unbecoming face, false teeth, false hair, and simulated height? Indeed, we might even wish her dead.

Nature has provided the minds of men with great diligence and a great love of truth. We are taken by truth and drawn to it; we think everything else should take second place to it and nobody is so stupid that he wants to be led into error willingly or through flattery. Who would allow himself to be deluded by deception or blinded by concealment? Who would not burn with anger when he feels that his face has been ill represented? Well then, I say that an adulterated translation is most like that kind of mirror, or like a woman's face plastered with cosmetics. Such a translation endows the author with the type of elegance that is not appropriate to his style: it fattens up what was thin, so to speak, it deflates what was bombastic, it raises up what was low, and brings low what was high. Let us suppose that somebody wants to translate Thucydides, an author who obviously knows how to deal with words, a man who writes in the grand style, concise and full of memorable phrases, swift, abrupt, and sometimes obscure – at least that is what Cicero calls him. Let us further suppose that the translator is a man of many words by nature, but also impartial, sincere, and capable of sweet eloquence. Thucydides' vehemence will be weakened, his obscurities will be clarified, and his recondite phrases will be watered down in the text's abundant flow. The translator will add ornaments generously and liberally, and he will bind the halting syntax of the original together with a rhythm of his own. Let us finally suppose that a reader who knows no Greek, but is eager to read Thucydides and to penetrate his inner recesses, picks up a translation of this kind. He will not find Thucydides in Thucydides, or else he will say that Thucydides has been turned into a fool by the translator. He will also doubt the honesty and judgment of Cicero and Fabius who maintain that Thucydides is a hermetic writer, stringent, always urging himself on, and richer in memorable phrases than in mere words.

Suppose somebody feels called upon to translate Xenophon, whose suave and brilliant style is praised by Cicero in so many words. Suppose the translator is a man of stern and austere disposition, who uses concise phrases and writes in a brief, sharp style which may therefore not appear open enough. Such a man will translate Xenophon not as he is, but as he wants him to be. He will not compose his own text after the manner of Xenophon, but rather the other way around. He will detract from the suave style of the original, add strength, and turn the Attic bee into an eagle. Whoever sees a Xenophon so reconstituted, wearing that kind of mask, will be sorely mistaken if he thinks he has seen the real Xenophon and taken him into his soul. I would, therefore, prefer to show Thucydides as a writer in the grand style, which he is, Xenophon as a suave and placid writer, Herodotus as candid and diffuse, and Isocrates as a man of many words, as far as possible. My Demosthenes would have to be lofty and solemn, my Plato exuberant, my Aristotle nervous, my Theophrastus sweet, and my Heraclitus obscure – especially if more of his writings had been preserved.

A translator must therefore become like Proteus: he must be able to transform himself into all manner of wondrous things, he must be able to absorb and combine all styles within himself and be more changeable than a chameleon. Suppose a well-read man, who has pleased the public with Cicero's wonderful wealth and abundance, begins to translate Aristotle, a writer who is sparse and dry, and begins to spin out in a Ciceronian manner what Aristotle wrote briefly and hermetically. We could not possibly hold the latter translation in high esteem. I have often asked myself from what source that license to corrupt older writers seems to spring, and it has occurred to me that the love for oneself which, as the Greeks have it, is innate in all men, linked with ignorance of the good, causes that kind of arrogance. As soon as this sort of illness insinuates itself into the minds of men, they will necessarily follow evil counsel, and that is where the temerity arises which this age has taken into itself, touching with its profane hands the works of the Ancients which should never be treated without respect, and hawking its own rubbish under their glorious names.

Let the translator be a severe judge for himself and let him not be too pleased to play the part of the judge too easily, even though he should arrive at a confident judgment of the author he sets out to translate. Translators often throw out what they do not understand, or even put in other things. If they retain what they do not grasp they often do so in such an ominous way that people who let the fetus of their own mind crawl into another's nest, where it often dislodges the rightful inhabitants, might still be called translators. To prevent such things from happening it is necessary to eradicate the opinion alive in people's minds that makes them claim to be better than they are. Everybody needs to correct the excesses of their style and everybody should approach old and foreign writings with great care. Everybody also needs to learn, to the very best of his ability, what a translator should be, and once he has learned that he should practice what he has learned in his own writing, and not allow his mind to interfere. Whoever acts differently is a mere busybody, not a translator, and we may say of him that he interpolates, not that he translates.

These, Casaubon, are my thoughts on the subject briefly stated. I have been entertaining these thoughts for quite a while, ever since I came across translations of the type just described, and I have come across quite a few, since many of them have been made in our own time. I have often regretted that unwary adolescence is so cunningly deluded, and when I realized what roads are open to the adolescent who wants to gain access to the holy sanctuaries of antiquity I have thrown obstacles in their way, and I have tried to close those roads with all my might. It is therefore a great joy for me to see not only that you are willing to stand up to this age, but also that you want to explore those closed roads and that you have even dared to open them to others. That task was destined to be yours if any man's, since you were so splendidly educated in Greek and Latin literature, not to mention the literatures of other nations. You have all of antiquity in your memory, you have the ability to translate and, what is most important, you are endowed with the kind of judgment that is sharp and not corrupt. I am afraid to go on praising you in your presence since you might think it more important to agree with me than to persevere in the task I am grateful to you for undertaking. Go on, therefore, and lay down rules if you want the translator to be the author's eternal imitator, if you want him to walk in the author's footsteps and if you want him to submit to his author by rendering the number of words his author uses by means of the same number of words.

CASAUBON: I was ready to do so, most distinguished Thuanus, but you thought of so many of these things before I did. You must therefore hear from me what is not obvious to everyone: I will say that you, out of thousands, have been my example – the very words Plato used to describe the poet Antimachus Clarius – if we can believe the tradition. I would therefore like to state that one should always translate word for word, and that one should preserve the syntax of the original text in as far as the languages the translator uses allow it. Should it happen that Greek words are such that one word in Greek does not always correspond to one word in Latin, then you can indeed bring in another word, or even more than one, if that is possible. Similarly, if you are translating from Greek and you find that the Latin language cannot occupy the positions Greek words occupy in the sentence, you are of course allowed to change the order of the words. The difference between languages, their density and their incompatibility can also create problems, except where the translator gets closer to the traces his author has left and explains him more clearly. I want the translator to follow in the author's footsteps and to cling to him so closely that the roads he travels are open and visible to all. Should those roads appear to be narrow, or rough, so that the translator who travels with his author is wrenched away from his guide, let him then take the nearest way into the thick of things, even if it is hard and difficult to do, and let him rather enter into briars and penetrate into places covered with thorns than look for an easy escape. If I see that the author has been shorn by the translator, and punished, it may be that the sentence I am looking for may have been cut, or maybe only one little word was cut, but it was the one that happened to bear the whole momentum of the sentence. If the author writes a simple style to start with and if that style is heightened with ornament I shall be seizing a body and holding on to a shadow, and if I think I am imitating the author I shall be following the translator. It must therefore be generally made

known that one word should be rendered by one word in translation and that the order of the words should not be wantonly
disturbed. But if that is obvious to everyone and if you had been
expecting something clearer from me, and more subtly argued, I
shall try to satisfy your wishes as best I can.

First, the translator must pay attention to the subject matter
treated by the author since the translation must be in accordance
with the kind of subject matter treated in the original. Saint
Jerome says that one word should be translated by one word in
Holy Writ, *where even the order of the words is a mystery*, where a
construction that has not been refined with great art often carries
more than one sentence. Since the greater part of Holy Writ
should not be studied for its elegance, however, Saint Jerome also
admits that other texts should be translated in a different manner,
nor does he always follow his own precepts. I too say that the
translator of Holy Writ should translate word for word. If current
and colloquial expressions are not sufficient he should resort to
obsolete words no longer in current usage. If those are not
available either the translator should have the audacity to invent
words nobody has heard before, provided he does so sparingly, of
course, and with great reserve. In that case the license he displays
will be worthy of praise. He should also preserve the word order
and not be deterred by obscurities and imperfections in his
composition. But if it happens that certain words cannot be
translated they will have to be invented. I want even the articles
translated with great care wherever they make the slightest difference, even though they are not all that important in a language.

I insist on treating Holy Writ with such care and diligence
because I do not want these oracles of the Holy Ghost to be
adulterated by human and earth-bound elements. For it is not
without divine counsel that they have been expressed in certain
words selected from a certain sphere and arranged in a certain
order, since there are as many mysteries hidden in them as there
are dots in the text. And did not Christ himself say that not one dot
should be erased from the law until heaven and earth are destroyed? So the man who would try to disturb those divine works
would be bold and overconfident indeed in trying to defile that
sacred vessel with the dregs of human ignorance. I would insist on
similar and almost equal fidelity in translations of the Church
Fathers and the theologians since the precepts of the Christian
faith are handed down in them, the dogmas of the faith and the

sacred shrines containing the words of the Lord. All those are hard to understand in their own right and require much effort. Any fall would be precipitous and the translator would find himself on uncertain ground if he had the audacity to delete certain words, add others, disturb the word order, or substantially change the style. We know that a contorted syllable, a letter that has been misplaced, a dot moved from its proper position have given rise to pestiferous heresies and we have heard that frequent errors have been produced by ambiguous diction. It is advisable, therefore, to consult with others when you try to explain the writings of the Fathers, especially their abstruse passages, and no vile translator should pollute these clearest wellsprings of holy knowledge with the mud of profane eloquence. Indeed, if the translator displays obscure zeal and inappropriate eloquence he might infect his readers with the virus of a damnable doctrine. Erasmus, a very learned man whose knowledge is not disputed by anyone, has shown the greatest sensibility to all of this. "I have always," he says, "tried to achieve a faithful and erudite simplicity in translating, especially in translating Holy Writ." We should therefore treat most holy theology and the fragments of Holy Writ contained in the pages of the Fathers with utmost care, and we should forbid any license in a translator, as in a pretty and modest virgin, as we try to stamp out impudence in intemperate men.

We are admonished to do so in theology by religion and the dignity of the subject matter. The degree of difficulty displayed by theoretical works counsels us to follow the same course since they, too, are replete with precepts. For subtle things, if I may speak with Horace, that have been expressed in subtle ways by the old writers, should also be rendered in subtle translations, not in a plethora of words. Indeed, who would want to embellish Aristotle's *Metaphysics* with words and phrases, Euclid's *Geometry*, Diophanes' books on mathematics, the *Harmony* of Aristoxenes, Apollonius' *Trigonometry*, or Galen's books on therapy and anatomy? Who would want them to be filled with flourishes of eloquence and abundance of words? Who would be able to listen to Archimedes reciting his works on spheres and cylinders in a poetical manner, or Ptolemy perorating on the movements of the stars without bursting into gales of laughter? *The subject matter itself does not need to be embellished: it just needs to be taught.* And it is quite obvious that it cannot be taught if it is full of embellishments which, like weeds that are the enemies of grains, will kill the good crops when sown in fertile fields. But you say I should speak at greater length about this to provide more illustrations. What if I were to act like an annotator or a paraphrast, not a translator? Who would know whether I followed my author's mind? Suppose a word is ambiguous and allows for a double interpretation. Why then only give one and not the other? If we follow your opinion what room is there left for conjecture or private judgment? If the author has left a concept suspended between two interpretations it should certainly be kept that way. An ambiguous word should be translated by another ambiguous word and the phrase's very ambiguity should be obvious in the translation.

FRONTO: But if a translator is to translate such a word in such a manner we shall never find out.

CASAUBON: We are not all that strict, my dear Fronto, we are willing to accept excuses, but we do not allow the translator to get away with everything and we don't want to be subjected to the way some people translate. If they have to translate a joke into another language and if the joke is based on a pun, a play on words, or ambiguity, they desert their author and make up a new pun, a new play on words, or a new ambiguity in the other language. We want the jokes your author made, my dear translator, not yours. And how do we get them? Like this: the word itself must be rendered faithfully and the meaning contained in it must be briefly explained in a footnote. If you do that you will have shown that you can be faithful to both the author and the reader. You will also produce almost no translations, no matter how accurate or well made, without the aid of notes or explanations, simply because languages are different. If the translation is stuffed full of notes and explanations it becomes an example of the weaknesses and aporias besetting translation itself. Let me, at this point, pay homage to my friend Henricus Stephanus, who spoke with great erudition of the old Romans whose diligence and wit enriched the Latin language. When they were faced with a word that had multiple meanings in their translations from the Greek, they simply attributed all those meanings to the corresponding Latin word. What they dared in their own language we should do very sparingly in a foreign language in which we do not feel at home, as well as in our own, unless usage prompts us to do so, *and the verdict should be left to taste and the power and norms of speech.*

But ambiguous words and other words of that ilk appear very rarely in the theoretical writings we are talking about. They occur much more often in the writings of historians and orators we shall be considering next, after we devote a few words to the grammarians. What has been said above should make the way in which grammarians should be translated abundantly clear. As we stated in our precepts the translator should reject all ornamentation. If he wants to translate the grammarians he should write in a clear and simple style, and that holds true also for other technical texts defining the rules of any given discipline.

Translators should also be careful not to resort to interpolations in books written by historians because they obscure the truth with alluring words, but it is the translator's duty to render the truth in its entirety. As I have said before, the characteristic features of all these authors need to be retained in such a way that they also shine through in the translation, as much as possible, except where they will be obliterated by the discrepancy in languages.

We are now left with the orators and the poets. Where the orators are concerned, I think the translator should be allowed to display a little license in one passage, and a little more in another, and you should not be offended by this show of great leniency on my part. The art of the orators consists not only of the splendor of their subject matter, but also of the skillful way in which they manage words, and there may be such masters of the word among them *that their mosaic is beautified by art, even if the individual pieces are eaten by worms.* The translator should first look at the subject matter, which is always the supreme rule. Next he should try to render the characteristic florid, sonorous, and artful style. He might succeed in the case of complete sentences, but not often. He might also succeed without adding any words of his own, but then he will be able to cut to the quick even less often. In most cases he will only succeed if he changes the order of the words somewhat. That order should be retained if it represents the same arrangement of words in both languages. If that is not the case, preserving the order of the words would reduce the original's artful composition to nothing. The orator has worked very hard to achieve a certain effect and if a slight change in the arrangement of the words is not made, the oration itself will become diffuse, lose its strength and turn into something fluid and shapeless – such is the curse of the difference between languages. Word order is not of such overriding importance that we should dissolve the well-structured composition achieved by the skillful orator to save it, since it is precisely that composition which is largely responsible for the oration's perfection.

We can grant the same license to translators who translate poets, since poets are so close to orators. We are justified in doing so because poets are bound to stricter numbers and a preestablished model of syllables. Such a text can be rendered into another language either directly or indirectly. If it is translated indirectly it will be tied to another form, in which case none of what we said before will be applicable. In this case the difference between languages should not be taken as an excuse to translate line by line in order to preserve the laws of translation. On the contrary, the translator needs to be able to make longish excursions and to write in different genres and forms.

If poets are translated in the first way there is no reason why they should not be translated word for word as long as we remember that these precepts should be forgotten when we are dealing with lines. If poets are translated in the second way the most important rule is to preserve the meter and the syntax, so that the poet can be shown to his new audience like a tree whose leaves have been removed by the rigors of winter, while the branches, the roots, and the trunk can still be seen. The translator's audacity should not be feared overmuch in this since most of the Greek authors have been translated accurately enough in this way. When Humfredus criticizes this way of translating in his commentary on the various ways of translating, he himself should be criticized for failing to understand that the translator who is supposed to translate in the manner he advocates, cannot possibly imitate the native charm that is to be found in Homer, or any other poet, if he is bound to the words. He would, in the end, have to render the original in a false manner, decked out with frigid and inelegant ornaments. Jerome does not distinguish with enough care between these two kinds of translation, strict and loose, and neither does Italus Catena who tried to defend our precepts of translation in his learned dissertation. They both used some older translations of poets as examples, but those translations have nothing to do with the matter in hand.

My learned friends, I have explained to you the precepts I think should govern the production of the best possible translations, and I have tried to support those precepts with arguments so that you may approve of them. If my speech is to proceed in the manner and the order established by the traditions of old, which we subscribe to, we must now pause to see if there is anything you want to say, or if I have spoken at too great length.

THUANUS: Your speech could never be too long for us, Casaubon, and I know I can speak for Fronto as well in this. You always hold forth in such a way that there is no room for doubt, and you have done so today as well. Speaking for myself I would be overwhelmed by your authority even if you had not used any arguments at all. But suppose someone else went up against you, an opinionated man who stuck to prejudice. It could then appear as if a few points were missing from what you said before. You probably wanted to explain them before when you confessed you were in doubt as to whether to say more or not.

CASAUBON: What do you have in mind?

THUANUS: You will hear it faster if you keep silent. That fictitious opponent of yours might say that your precepts carry little weight since you yourself did not observe them in your translation of Polybius, and even less so in your translation of Theophrastus's *Characters*. He might add that you followed your authors loosely, not strictly, and certainly not word for word, and that you revealed yourself their eternal, more or less faithful servant. He might also add that this attitude does not tally with what you have decreed and that it would never become possible to render the characteristic features of an author if word is to be measured against word and if the word order is to be preserved in both languages. What may be a pleasant arrangement of words in Greek may turn out to be inelegant, halting, and diluted in Latin. You must therefore either leave the words, the syllables and their order alone, or you must omit your author's very form and innate quality. Furthermore, your imaginary opponent might go on to accuse you of not being too strict or rigorous yourself, while promulgating laws more stringent than Draco's, or the decrees

Manlius issued. He might go on to say that nobody can obey those laws, no matter how obedient or compliant a person he is, certainly not in cases where the two languages are so different from each other in the number of words and their meaning, in the differences between their genders, cases, and meters, in the abundance and inflection of their articles, nouns, and pronouns, in the multitude of their conjugations, in the plenitude of their words, and in a number of other analogous points. Greek and French abound in articles, Latin has none. These three languages have few conjugations compared to Hebrew, not to mention Arabic. Greek has the aorist and the active participle of the past tense, both of which are lacking in Latin. No power of the intellect, no matter how great, no skill in handling a language and no familiarity with it can lead to perfect results as long as the translator does not decide to leave the author by the wayside in many instances. Finally, there are certain phrases specific to each language (grammarians call them idioms) that would be utterly ridiculous if transposed into another language, or else they would create more ambiguities that could be avoided only if the transla-tor were to resort to long circumlocutions. I think if a translator were to render Greek proverbs literally into French he would be considered a fool and become the laughing-stock of all who read him. Jerome himself said that

> It is difficult not to cut here and there when following lines written by another, and it is hard to preserve the elegance with which things have been expressed in the original when you are writing a translation. A given word may mean a very specific thing in one language and I may not have a word to render it with in another, and while I ponder how to fill in its sense, I may be confusing a narrow space with a long winding road. Add to this the digressions caused by rhetoric, the differences in declensions, the number of stylistic features and, finally, the feature which sets each individual language apart, its genius, as they say. If I translate word for word all this will sound ridiculous, but if I am forced to change something in the syntax, or in the text, I may give the impression that I am neglecting the task of the translator.

This statement is an obvious refutation of yours. And then there is also what Jerome writes to Rufinus: "If any metaphor is literally translated from one language into another, the seeds of the text and its sense will be suffocated by brambles, as it were." The discrepancies between all languages are not the same and Latin is further removed from Hebrew, because of its verb system, than it is from Greek. The same law can therefore not be valid for all translations. Moreover, nobody is so coarse and so stupid in his taste that he would touch such a word for word translation, even if it reads fluently, since it will be so boorish and crude that it is bound to make him feel nauseous. When a reader begins to read it with the honest intention of persevering to the end, he will soon find himself yawning as a certain languor creeps up on him, coupled with a certain disgust, and he will hardly be able to keep sleep at bay. The translator who religiously refuses to change even the smallest dot in his author, will destroy that author by producing such an inept translation. The fruits promised and expected after so much diligence on the translator's part will be cut off, and yet how would their abundance not have been praised if the translation had been pleasing to the ear. This stubborn detractor of yours might marshal these and other arguments of the same kind against the rules you have proposed, and I am waiting eagerly for you to refute him.

CASAUBON: The knowledge that you are friendly to our cause, my illustrious Thuanus, gives me the confidence to sustain the attack of the opponent you impersonate. If I should falter, I shall remember that you promised to swell the ranks of my followers, and I myself will take you for my helper. I shall elude the attack I have been challenged to simply by executing a small feint to the side: when we started this conversation you asked me what I thought would be the best way to translate, not how I myself translate. Whenever you speak about a discipline, you usually speak in general terms, stating the ideal and the absolute. The translator I spoke of may very well never have existed, nor may he ever exist in the future, and you did not ask me to show him to you, nor anybody like him. I have therefore made up a perfect model of a translator, a model awaiting imitation by those who would turn their hearts to the discipline of translating. What I desire in others I myself have tried to achieve as best I could, and if I have not reached perfection I am at least able to point out where I have come close to it in my Polybius translation. I will say more, since I have nothing to hide. I have sometimes struck a compromise with the age I live in for I, too, have seen and experienced what is better but I, too, have sometimes done what is worse. I have tried nearly everywhere to bring the Latin and the Greek into harmony. My next care has been to be true to the Latin as much as I could, so that I might not appear to indulge in idle boasting in that long letter in which I dedicated the whole work to our great king. Your opponent also attacks me for another reason, namely that the rules we have promulgated are mutually incoherent since the translator cannot at the same time retain the structure and the order of the words and display the author's characteristic features – and yet I want him to do both. It is easy for me to conduct a brief defense of my own person in this matter: every language has its own characteristics, its own genius, so to speak, which is not found in other languages. Your opponent, Thuanus, has rightly perceived this, since a word order that may express something splendid and sonorous in Hebrew may sound low and humble in Latin. If the translator tries to preserve all this, so that nothing leaks away, he will be like Lysippus who wanted to sculpt Alexander's countenance in bronze and tried to find ways to show the color of his cheeks, the softness of his skin, his warmth, the breath that came out of his mouth and the movement of his lips and eyelashes. We would be in the best of all possible worlds if we could translate in both the ways described above. It is right to strive for the best, or to hope for it at least, but in most cases we must be satisfied with a translation that has been made in either of the two ways. So, to go back to the example I just gave, Lysippus decided not to worry about all the things his art could not achieve and to direct all his energy to rendering the collocation, the dimension, and the harmony of all the parts in one way only. This is how he made the likeness, and once he had expressed these features to perfection, the figure itself and its character would show in the face or the mouth. In the same way the translator must pursue the meaning of words and their composition. Once he has rendered these as diligently as he can, his author's character will show itself in such a way that it can be guessed from the contours even if it is not accurately expressed. I insist that the translator should reproduce the construction of the words and the form, or style, of the original because I want to repress that foolish license in those people who run the most disparate styles together into one and the same, most probably their own, whether that is facile and diffuse or grand and concise. As a result they impose books on us they think of as good, but that are the worst possible translations, in my opinion.

THUANUS: And would we not be better off if we had the worst books imposed on us, rather than the best translations?

CASAUBON: Are you trying to say that a good translation could not be a good book? I say and maintain that the most important rule is to first get to know the author and his illustrious character through your own powers of intuition, and then to express those. I have also taught that the translator might be able to do so more easily if he does not move away from the words, as far as possible, since that is the safest way to express the author's way of writing, his form, his style, or his character. The opponent you pit against me should also notice how subtly and cautiously I have distinguished between the various ways of translating, depending on author and subject matter. Whoever wants to translate Holy Writ must weigh word against word and ignore the style of the original that will shine forth well enough either in the way the words are matched or in the overall effect the translation makes.

I have also insisted on the word, rather than the style, in the case of the Church Fathers, the philosophers, the mathematicians, and the technical writers, and all those who write with great subtlety about many subjects. Their style constitutes itself in the number and order of their words, and those words will not be matched in a translation that imitates the style first, while not even translating it. I cannot insist on the same requirements in the case of orators, which is why I have been so benign and liberal where they are concerned. As to the poets: since their text can never retain the same poetic style in translation, as soon as it has been freed of its meter, I fail to see why the translation should stretch itself to conform to the original. When a corrector inserts stricter and more astringent features the text is made harder and less fluent, since there is no way *to make a bad text worse, and he cuts out what is good to save what is bad.* Such is the rule we want the translator to follow if the language he makes use of allows it. If I were to expect a man who translates into Latin to produce Greek aorists, or those multiple conjugations one finds in Hebrew or Arabic, I would be unjust and inexperienced. If a word occurs for which the translator cannot find an exact equivalent I want him to invent as few new words as possible. I would allow that practice only occasionally, when one translates Holy Writ, and then only if there is an urgent need for it.

Whenever similar difficulties occur in other texts the translator should resort to words related in meaning, or even to paraphrase, as long as he does not do so in an outrageous manner. If he is faced with an idiom or a metaphor I do not want him to mix in another proverb or another metaphor. He should render the words as they are and if their meaning is ambiguous he should briefly explain it in the margin or in footnotes, as I said before. If he fails to do so he will find himself moving farther and farther away from the author, because of the difference in their languages. As to the sleepy, yawning reader you referred to at the end of your remarks: I do not like those delicate, fastidious men whose palate cannot be pleased except by cakes and sweetmeats, sesame, poppies, wheat, and crushed nuts. I do not think only adolescents in schools grow dumb on those things as Petronius Arbiter pointed out. I think the same thing happens to men of a mature age and a stupid, puerile disposition. If you are depressed and have a sour stomach, don't blame the food. These are the arguments I had gathered, my dear Thuanus, to refute our opponent's attack and his subtle machinations. If he wants to insist we need not despair in our souls.

John Dryden, 1631–1700. English poet, dramatist, critic, and translator.

Extracts from the preface to his translation of *Ovid's Epistles* published in 1680.

All translation, I suppose, may be reduced to these three heads.

First, that of metaphrase, or turning an author word by word, and line by line, from one language into another. Thus, or near this manner, was Horace his *Art of Poetry* translated by Ben Jonson. The second way is that of paraphrase, or translation with latitude, where the author is kept in view by the translator, so as never to be lost, but his words are not so strictly followed as his sense; and that too is admitted to be amplified, but not altered. Such is Mr. Waller's translation of Virgil's Fourth *Aeneid*. The third way is that of imitation, where the translator (if now he has not lost that name) assumes the liberty, not only to vary from the words and sense, but to forsake them both as he sees occasion; and taking only some general hints from the original, to run division on the groundwork, as he pleases. Such is Mr. Cowley's practice in turning two Odes of Pindar, and one of Horace, into English.

The verbal copier is encumbered with so many difficulties at once, that he can never disentangle himself from all. He is to consider, at the same time, the thought of his author, and his words, and to find out the counterpart to each in another language; and, besides this, he is to confine himself to the compass of numbers, and the slavery of rhyme. 'Tis much like dancing on ropes with fettered legs: a man may shun a fall by using caution; but gracefulness of motion is not to be expected: and when we have said the best of it, 'tis but a foolish task; for no sober man would put himself into a danger for the applause of escaping without breaking his neck.

The consideration of these difficulties, in a servile, literal translation, not long since made two of our famous wits, Sir John Denham and Mr. Cowley, to contrive another way of turning authors into our tongue, called, by the latter of them, imitation. As they were friends, I suppose they communicated their thoughts on this subject to each other; and therefore their reasons for it are little different, though the practice of one is much more moderate. I take imitation of an author, in their sense, to be an endeavour of a later poet to write like one who has written before him, on the same subject; that is, not to translate his words, or to be confined to his sense, but only to set him as a pattern, and to write, as he supposes that author would have done, had he lived in our age, and in our country. Yet I dare not say, that either of them have carried this libertine way of rendering authors (as Mr. Cowley calls it) so far as my definition reaches; for in the *Pindaric Odes* the customs and ceremonies of ancient Greece are still preserved. But I know not what mischief may arise hereafter from the example of such an innovation, when writers of unequal parts to him shall imitate so bold an undertaking. To add and to diminish what we please, which is the way avowed by him, ought only to be granted to Mr. Cowley, and that too only in his translation of Pindar; because he alone was able to make him amends, by giving him better of his own, whenever he refused his author's thoughts. Pindar is generally known to be a dark writer, to want connection (I mean as to our understanding), to soar out of sight, and leave his reader at a gaze. So wild and ungovernable a poet cannot be translated less literally; his genius is too strong to bear a chain, and Samson-like he shakes it off. A genius so elevated and unconfined as Mr. Cowley's, was but necessary to make Pindar speak English, and that was to be performed by no other way than imitation. But if Virgil, or Ovid, or any regular intelligible authors, be thus used, 'tis no longer to be called their work, when neither the thoughts nor words are drawn from the original; but instead of them there is something new produced, which is almost the creation of another hand. By this way, 'tis true, somewhat that is excellent may be invented, perhaps more excellent than the first design; though Virgil must be still excepted, when that *perhaps* takes place. Yet he who is inquisitive to know an author's thoughts will be disappointed in his expectation; and 'tis not always that a man will be content to have a present made him, when he expects the payment of a debt. To state it fairly: imitation of an author is the most advantageous way for a translator to show himself, but the greatest wrong which can be done to the memory and reputation of the dead. Sir John Denham (who advised more liberty than he took himself) gives his reason for his innovation, in his admirable Preface before the translation of the Second *Aeneid*: *Poetry is of so subtile a spirit, that, in pouring out of one language into another, it will all evaporate; and if a new spirit be not added in the transfusion, there will remain nothing but a caput mortuum.* I confess this argument holds good against a literal translation; but who defends it? Imitation and verbal version are, in my opinion, the two extremes which ought to be avoided; and therefore, when I have proposed the mean betwixt them, it will be seen how far his argument will reach.

No man is capable of translating poetry, who, besides a genius to that art, is not a master both of his author's language, and of his own; nor must we understand the language only of the poet, but his particular turn of thoughts and expression, which are the characters that distinguish, and as it were individuate him from all other writers. When we are come thus far, 'tis time to look into ourselves, to conform our genius to his, to give his thought either the same turn, if our tongue will bear it, or, if not, to vary but the dress, not to alter or destroy the substance. The like care must be taken of the more outward ornaments, the words. When they appear (which is seldom) literally graceful, it were an injury to the author that they should be changed. But since every language is so full of its own properties, that what is beautiful in one, is often barbarous, nay sometimes nonsense, in another, it would be unreasonable to limit a translator to the narrow compass of his author's words: 'tis enough if he choose out some expression which does not vitiate the sense. I suppose he may stretch his chain to such a latitude; but by innovation of thoughts, methinks he breaks it. By this means the spirit of an author may be transfused, and yet not lost: and thus 'tis plain that the reason alleged by Sir John Denham has no farther force than to expression; for thought, if it be translated truly, cannot be lost in another language; but the words that convey it to our apprehension (which are the image and ornament of that thought), may be so ill chosen, as to make it appear in an unhandsome dress, and rob it of its native lustre. There is, therefore, a liberty to be allowed for the expression; neither is it necessary that words and lines should be confined to the measure of their original. The sense of an author, generally speaking, is to be sacred and inviolable. If the fancy of Ovid be luxuriant, 'tis his character to be so; and if I retrench it, he is no longer Ovid. It will be replied, that he receives advantage by this lopping of his superfluous branches; but I rejoin, that a translator has no such right. When a painter copies from the life, I suppose he has no privilege to alter features and lineaments, under pretence that his picture will look better: perhaps the face which he has drawn would be more exact, if the eyes or nose were altered; but 'tis his business to make it resemble the original. In two cases only there may a seeming difficulty arise; that is, if the thought be notoriously trivial or dishonest; but the same answer will serve for both, that then they ought not to be translated.

Jean le Rond d'Alembert, 1717–1783. French philosopher and mathematician. Leading figure in the French Enlightenment movement.

Extracts from the "Observations sur l'art de traduire" ("Remarks on the Art of Translating") that constitute the preface to his translation of Tacitus, published in 1758.

It is not my intention to dictate any laws. Those among our good writers who have practiced the art of translation with success would have more right to pose as legislators, but they have done better than to transcribe rules: they have given examples. Let us study the art in their work and not in a few questionable decisions they have made, which are the object of dispute. For what precepts are preferable to the study of great models? The latter always enlighten, the former sometimes hinder. In all modes of writing reason has given a small number of rules, whim has extended them, and from them pedantry has forged the irons prejudice respects and talent dares not break. Wherever you turn in the realm of the arts you will see mediocrity laying down the law and genius stooping to obey. Genius is a sovereign imprisoned by slaves. Yet, although he should not allow himself to be subjugated, he should also not be allowed to do everything he likes. In my opinion this rule, so essential for the progress of literature, should be applied not only to original works, but also to works of imitation, such as translation. Let me therefore try, in this essay, to avoid the twin excesses of rigidity and indulgence that are equally dangerous. I shall first examine the laws of translation with respect to the nature of languages; then I shall examine those laws as far as they deal with the genius of writers; and finally I shall examine those laws with respect to the conventions that can be established in this mode of writing.

It is commonly believed that the art of translation would be the easiest of all to practice, if only one language corresponded exactly to another. If that were the case, I venture to think there would be many more mediocre translators, and far fewer excellent ones. Translators of the first kind would limit themselves to a slavishly literal translation and they would be unable to see anything beyond that. Translators of the second kind would also want to include harmony and facility of style, two qualities good writers have never neglected; in fact, they even constitute the main characteristics of the work done by a few among them. The translator therefore needs to judge with extreme care in which cases exact perfection of resemblance gives way to elegance of diction without being weakened too much. One of the main problems in the art of writing, and especially in translation, is to judge the extent to which one is allowed to sacrifice energy to nobility, correctness to invention, and rigorous precision to the mechanisms of style. Reason is a stern judge and we must stand in awe of it; the ear is a proud judge and we had better not offend it. It would therefore be best not to establish literal translation as a rule, not even where the nature of the languages does not seem to be adverse to it and where the translation will turn out to be dry, hard, and unharmonious anyway.

Be that as it may, the difference in the nature of languages almost never allows for literal translations and so frees the translator from the dilemma just mentioned, namely the obligation to sometimes sacrifice pleasure to precision or precision to pleasure. On the other hand, the very fact that he cannot possibly render the original feature by feature leaves the translator with a dangerous freedom. Since he cannot endow the copy with a perfect resemblance, he must take care to endow it with the full resemblance it will allow for. Anyway, if the fine points of our own language demand so much study before we can know them thoroughly, how much more effort is required to disentangle the nuances of a foreign language, and what is a translator to do without that double knowledge?

One might be tempted to think that some translators need not worry too much on this account, and I am thinking here of those who translate the classics. If the finer points of diction in the original are not clear to the translators, they will not be clear to their critics either. Yet, through some strange quirk of fate, those translators are subjected to harsher treatment than others. The superstitions we harbor about antiquity make us believe that the classics always expressed themselves in the most felicitous manner. In short, our ignorance is advantageous to the model, to the detriment of the copy. The translator always appears to be below the perception the original projects of itself, but not below the perception we have of it. To round off the contradiction, we also admire those of our contemporaries who write in Latin. Most of them, who write insipid stuff in their own language, impress us beyond measure in a language that no longer exists. We do to languages what we do to writers: we pay them tribute as soon as they are dead.

But is it really true that languages are different in nature? I am not ignorant of the fact that contemporary men of letters who pride themselves on their philosophical spirit, and even show some on occasion, have maintained the opposite. This absurd opinion has, in turn, been blamed on the philosophical spirit, which had nothing whatsoever to do with it. In the hands of a writer of genius all languages no doubt lend themselves to all styles: they will be light or pathetic, naive or sublime as author and theme require. In that sense languages do not exhibit distinguishing features. But if they can all be used for the same type of work they cannot all be used to express the same idea. Herein lies the diversity of their genius.

As a consequence of that diversity languages tend to exhibit advantages and disadvantages when compared to each other. Their advantages will be greater when they have more variety in phraseology and more brevity in construction, when they have more freedom and more richness. A language is not rich because it is able to express one and the same idea by means of an abundance of synonyms, but because it is able to express every nuance of a concept by means of different terms.

Of all modern languages cultivated by men of letters Italian is the most versatile, the most flexible, the most pliable to the shapes one wants to impose on it. It is therefore as rich in good translations as it is in excellent vocal music, which is itself another form of translation. Our language, on the other hand, is the strictest of all in its laws, the most uniform in its construction, and the most inhibited in its flow. Small wonder that it should be a cliff on which both poets and translators founder. But what should that teach us? We should learn to hold our good authors in higher esteem since they do not have the power to deliver us of mediocrities.

Languages have their own genius; so do writers. The original's distinguishing features must therefore be transferred to the copy. This rule is both the most highly recommended and the least practiced, and readers themselves give proof of the greatest indulgence where it is concerned. How many translations represent the most disparate works of literature in the same way, like beautiful women with regular features but without a soul or physiognomy of their own? There, if I may say so, is the kind of absurdity that hurts translations most. Other mistakes pass and correct themselves but this one is continuous and without remedy. The blots you can make disappear by rubbing them out almost do not deserve that name. Mistakes do not kill a translation; the chill does. Translations are nearly always more defective on account of what is not there than on account of what the author did put in.

Representing the original in a translation is all the more difficult because the characteristics of that original are often easily misinterpreted, and it is often easy to see only one facet of it. A writer may have a double feature in his style, concision, and vividness, for one must not believe that these two qualities necessarily go together since brevity may also be grouped with coldness and dryness. Yet a translator will be satisfied with conciseness in trying to resemble the author we are talking about. If he is concise without being vivid he will have missed the most precious part of the likeness.

But how do you take on foreign characteristics if nature has not prepared you for them? Writers of genius should, therefore, be translated only by those who are like them and are content to be their imitators while they could be their rivals. It is said that a painter who is mediocre in his own work may excel in the copies he makes. To do so the painter only needs to follow the path of servile instruction; the translator, on the other hand, copies with his own colors.

A writer's characteristic features reside either in his thinking or in his style, or both. Writers whose characteristic features reside in their thinking suffer the smallest losses when they are transferred into another language. Corneille ought therefore to be easier to translate than Racine and (even though this may seem paradoxical) translating Tacitus should be easier than translating Sallust. Sallust says everything, but with few words, a positive feature not easily kept in translation. Tacitus leaves much to be inferred and he makes his readers think, a positive feature the translator cannot afford to lose in translation.

Writers who combine elegance of ideas with elegance of style offer more resources to the translator than those who please through their style only. In the first case the translator may flatter himself with the thought that he succeeds in transferring the characteristic features of the author's thinking to the copy and, consequently, that he succeeds in transferring at least half of the author's spirit. In the second case he succeeds in rendering nothing if he fails to render diction.

In this last class of writers, who present the translator with a more thankless task than all the others, the least rebellious are those whose principal distinguishing feature is that they wield their language in an elegant manner, while the more intractable are those who have their own way of writing. It is possible that the English may have succeeded in translating a few of Racine's tragedies. I doubt that they would be able to translate La Fontaine's *Fables* with the same kind of success since this is probably the most original work the French language has ever produced. They would also be hard pressed to translate the *Aminta*, a pastoral work full of those gallant details and pleasant baubles Italian is so good at that they should be left in that language.

Finally, they would not find it easy to translate the letters of Madame de Sévigné, so frivolous in their essence and so seductive in the very negligence with which their style is handled. Some foreigners have treated them with contempt because they did not know how to translate them. Indeed, nothing helps to dismiss problems faster than contempt does.

The question has been raised whether poets can be translated in verse, especially in our language, which does not admit of unrhymed verse, unlike English and Italian, and which allows no leeway to either the poet or the translator. Some of our writers have maintained that poets cannot be translated into prose, either because they like poetry or because they like problems. Prose translations, they add, would disfigure poets and deprive them of their principal charm, measure, and harmony. That still leaves the question of whether one is forced to imitate poets in verse, rather than translating them. The difference in harmony between the two languages alone represents an insurmountable difficulty for all verse translations. Can anyone seriously believe that our poetry with its rhymes, its half-lines that are always similar, the uniformity of its progression and its monotony – if one may say so – might be able to represent the varied cadences of Greek and Latin poetry? Yet the difference in harmony is the least of our difficulties. Let us ask those of our great poets who have successfully transferred some beautiful passages of Homer or Virgil into our language how often they have been forced to substitute equally felicitous ideas taken from their own resources for ideas they were unable to render, to substitute lines relying on feeling for lines relying on imagery, to substitute vividness of phrasing for energy of expression, to substitute verse relying on intellect for the pomp of harmony.

To translate a poet into prose is to change a measured aria into a recitative; to translate him into verse is to change one aria into another, which may be just as good, but is not the same. The one is a weak copy that exhibits a certain resemblance; the other is a work on the same subject and not a copy at all. But what do we have to do to get to know the poets who have written in a foreign language? Learn that language, of course.

What conclusions can we draw from these reflections? If we were to measure merit merely according to problems solved, we would often encounter fewer problems in creating literature than in translating it. In men of genius ideas are born without effort, and the expression most apt to render those ideas is born together with them. It is almost uniquely the task of the art of translation to express ideas that are not ours in a way that is, and that art is all the greater in that it cannot allow itself to be detected. Yet no matter how well it is hidden we always know it is there, and that is the reason why we prefer original work to imitation. Nature never loses the rights it has on us: the products it has made by itself always move us most deeply. We therefore prefer fruit grown in its native soil and nurtured with ordinary skill and mediocre care to fruit transplanted into that same soil with much toil and trouble. We will eat the latter on occasion, but we always go back to the former.

Yet while we award creative writers the first rank they deserve it would seem that an excellent translator should be ranked immediately below them, above writers who wrote as well as they could, but remained untouched by genius. But there is a certain fatalism among us that spreads to all the arts that rely on taking over foreign characteristics. There are those we have reviled with the most unjust prejudice; there are also those we do not give sufficient consideration, and the translator's work is among them.

It is not this injustice alone that makes the task so thankless and the number of translators so small. Even though they are faced with a number of bonds they cannot break when practicing their art, we have taken pleasure in tightening those bonds, as if we want to discourage them, even if we go against our own best interests in doing so.

The first yoke they allow to be put on them, or rather, put on themselves, is to limit themselves to being copiers rather than rivals of the writers they translate. They cling to their original with such superstitious dread that they would believe themselves guilty of sacrilege if they embellished it, even in its weak spots. They only allow themselves to be inferior to it and they succeed without any difficulty. It is more or less as if a skillful engraver, who copies the painting of a great master, would not allow himself a few light and graceful touches to enhance its beauty or mask its defects. Should the translator, so often forced to remain below his author, not place himself above him when he can? What about the objection that it is to be feared that such liberty will degenerate into license? If the original is well chosen there will not be much call for corrections or embellishments; if many of them are needed the original is not worth translating.

A second obstacle translators have put in their own paths is a shyness which holds them back when, with a little courage, they could lift themselves to the same level as their models. That courage consists of the willingness to coin new expressions to render certain vivid and energetic expressions found in the original. No doubt one should do this sparingly and only when necessary. And when is that? When the problem in translating is caused only by the genius of the languages? Each of them has its laws, and nobody is allowed to change them: to speak Latin in French would smack more of a bizarre enterprise than of a daring feat. But when you think the author has risked an expression of genius in his own language, you can start looking for analogous expressions. And what is an expression of genius? Not a new word, dictated by laziness or eccentricity, but rather the skillful and necessary joining of some known terms that allow for a new idea to be expressed in an energetic manner. This is almost the only type of innovation allowed in writing.

The most indispensable proviso accompanying those new expressions is that they should not suggest even the suspicion of constraint to the reader, even though that is precisely what caused their coinage. Sometimes you happen to meet very spirited foreigners who speak our language with great courage and great ease. When they converse with us they think in their own language and translate into ours, and we often regret that the energetic and singular terms they use are not sanctioned by common usage. As long as it is correct, the way these foreigners converse is the image of a good translation. The original must speak our own language in it, not with that superstitious shyness one feels for one's own language, but with that noble freedom that makes us borrow some features from one language to slightly embellish another. A translation will then possess all the qualities that make it worthy of esteem: the natural and easy look, the imprint of the genius of the original and, at the same time, that feel of the native soil any foreign tincture is bound to give it.

Well-made translations would therefore be the fastest and the surest way to enrich languages. This advantage would, it seems to me, be more real than the one ascribed to art by that famous satirist of the past century who was both a passionate admirer of the Ancients and a severe and sometimes unjust judge of the

Moderns. "The French," he used to say, "have no taste. Only classical taste is capable of forming writers and critics among us, and good translations would impart that precious taste to those who would not be able to read the originals." If we are lacking in taste I do not know where it has fled to. At least we are not lacking in it for lack of models in our own language, which are by no means inferior to the Ancients. Let us limit the comparison to dead authors and ask who would dare rank Sophocles higher than Corneille, Euripides higher than Racine, Theophrastus higher than La Bruyère, Phaedrus higher than La Fontaine? We should therefore not limit our classical library to translations, but we should not exclude them either. They are sure to multiply good models: they will help us to know the characteristic features of writers, peoples, and epochs; they will make us perceive the nuances that distinguish absolute and universal taste from what is merely national.

The third arbitrary law translators have been forced to obey is the ridiculous constraint of having to translate an author from A to Z. As a result the translator, weary and cold in the weak passages, languishes in the excellent ones. And why should he torture himself by rendering a false thought with elegance, or a common thought with wit? We do not transfer the classics into our language to familiarize ourselves with their defects but rather to enrich our literature with the best they have achieved. To translate them in extracts is not to mutilate them but rather to paint them in profile and to their advantage. What pleasure can one derive from the passage in which the Furies take away the Trojans' dinner in a translation of the *Aeneid*, from the cold and sometimes gross jokes disfiguring his speeches in a translation of Cicero, or from the passages in which some historian's narrative offers nothing of interest, either in substance or in style? Why, finally, transplant into a certain language what is graceful only in another, like the details of agriculture and pastoral life so pleasant in Virgil and so insipid in all prose translations? Or does Horace's eminently wise precept to abandon what you cannot do successfully not apply to translation as well as to other modes of writing?

Our men of letters would find it greatly to their advantage to translate extracts from certain works that contain enough beauty to bless many a writer with, and whose authors would erase those who now occupy first place if they had as much taste as they have wit. What pleasure could Seneca and Lucian not give if they had been tightened and thinned by a skillful translator? Seneca, so eminently quotable and so tiresome to read, who keeps spinning the same object around with dazzling speed, as opposed to Cicero who always advances toward his goal, but slowly. Lucian, the Seneca of poets, so full of male and true beauty, but too rhetorical, too monstrous, too full of maxims and empty of images. The only writers who would require a complete translation are those who give pleasure through their very negligence, as Plutarch does in his *Lives of Famous People*, in which he keeps dropping his subject matter only to pick it up again, and manages to pursue a conversation with his reader without tiring him out.

What I propose to do here, namely to translate the classics in the form of extracts, leads to another thought that is connected only indirectly with the matter in hand, to be sure, but which may turn out to be useful nonetheless. Our schools limit themselves to putting a small number of authors into the hands of our children and they usually show them only small portions taken from each author, to explicate and learn by heart. Their memory is indifferently filled with the good, the mediocre, and even the bad things these portions contain. Since most teachers tend to be somewhat deficient in taste, they hardly ever point out the really beautiful passages to their pupils; would it therefore not be infinitely more advantageous to select the very best passages from the different works of each author and to present to our children who read the classics only those portions deserving to be remembered? This way children would not assimilate everything the classics have thought, but they would assimilate the best. They would be familiar with the style and the genius of a greater number of writers. They would, at long last, have the opportunity of embellishing their mind while educating their taste. Such an anthology need not be immense if it is put together with discrimination, and the normal time allotted to study at school would be sufficient for students to become thoroughly familiar with it. We cannot exhort skillful men of letters enough to undertake this task, as long as they possess two qualities, the combination of which is rather rare, namely to be deeply versed in knowledge of the Ancients and, at the same time, to be free of any superstitious prejudice in their favor. They should not take after that ridiculous admirer of Homer who undertook to underline all the passages he thought admirable in that great poet and who, having read him for the third time, wound up underlining everything in his copy from A to Z. Could such a man flatter himself with the thought that he knew the real beauty of Homer and would Homer himself have been flattered with such an admirer?

I would be a fool to think that all readers would appreciate the strategy I have tried to follow in this translation. In this matter, more than in any other, every reader has his own measure, so to speak, and his own prejudices, if you like, and he wants the translator to live up to those. Nothing, therefore, is probably more rare in literature than a translation that is generally approved of. Even if it were approved of in its entirety, how many details would there not be left to criticize? I would be very happy if my translation were to meet with the approval of that small group of men of letters who have a deep knowledge of the nature of both languages, the genius of Tacitus himself, and the real rules of the art of translation: they should be able to appreciate my work. There are others who only think they have that knowledge; I have nothing to expect from them, nor do I require anything of them.

The only mercy I would like to be shown by those I recognize as my real judges would be that they not limit themselves to pointing out my mistakes, but that they also allow me to correct them once they have been pointed out to me. Of all the injustices translators have a right to complain about, and I have already described a few of them, the most glaring is the way in which they are usually criticized. I am not referring to vague, inept, disloyal criticism that should simply be disregarded, but I am referring to the kind of criticism that appears to be well-motivated, and even ostensibly just, and I maintain that it will not be sufficient in the case of translation. It is possible to judge an original work by limiting oneself to a well-argued criticism of the defects one notices in it because the author was the master of his plan, of what he had to say and of the way to say it, but the translator is forced to act under constraints on each of these counts. He is continually forced to follow a narrow and slippery road, not of his choice, and sometimes he has to throw himself to one side to avoid falling into the abyss. If one wants to criticize him in an equitable manner, therefore, one should not just point out that he has made some mistake; he must also be convinced of the fact that he could have done better, or at least as well, without making that mistake. It is pointless to tell a translator that his translation is lacking in rigorous exactness if you are unable to show him, at the same time, that he could have been exact without becoming less pleasing. It is pointless to maintain that he has not rendered the author's sense completely if you cannot prove to him that he could have done so without making the copy weak and flaccid. It is pointless to tell him that his translation is too audacious if you are unable to substitute another one for it, which is more natural and just as vigorous. To correct an author's blemishes is counted in favor of ordinary critics; it is the duty of those who criticize translations. Small wonder, therefore, that good criticism is even more rare than good original work in this mode of writing as in all others. And why should it not be? Satire is so easy! And the average reader does not even insist on its being at least a trifle witty. In the realm of literature satire ensures that you will be read. Whether you will also gain your reader's respect is another matter.

Charles Batteux, 1713–1780. French theoretician of literature and the arts.

Extracts from "De la construction oratoire" ("On Constructing Texts"), a chapter from *Principes de la littérature* ("Principles of Literature"), his main work on Poetics, published in 1777.

Only those who have never translated classical authors would doubt the difficulty of the enterprise. Those who have had the experience know that you often need more time, more effort, and more diligence to copy a beautiful painting than to create one.

When you translate the big problem is not to understand the author's thoughts. You can usually do so with the help of good editions and commentaries, and certainly if you examine the link between the thoughts. But the problem is to render things, thoughts, expressions, stylistic features, the general tone of the work and the particular tones of the particular styles of poets, orators, historians, and to render things as they are, without adding anything, moving anything, or taking anything away. The thoughts must be rendered with their colors, degrees, nuances. You must render the stylistic features that give fire, spirit, life to the discourse, as well as the expressions, natural or figurative, strong, rich, gracious, delicate. And you must do all this while trying to follow a model that commands without pity and wants to be obeyed with ease. It is obvious, therefore, that you need at least as much taste, if not as much genius, to translate well as you need to write well – or maybe more.

The author, guided by his genius that is always free and by his subject matter that presents him with ideas he may accept or reject as he pleases, is the absolute master of his thoughts and expressions. He is allowed to dismiss what he cannot express. The translator is master of nothing, he must bend with infinite suppleness to all the variations he finds in his author. Just consider the variety of tones that can be found within the same subject matter and, *a fortiori*, within the same genre. If the parts that make up the subject matter have been attuned and brought into proper harmony you can observe the rising and falling of the style and see how it grows softer and stronger, more or less constricted, without overreaching the unity of its fundamental character. Terence has a style that is suited to comedy all the way through. It is always simple and delicate, but it is so to different degrees whether spoken by Simon or Daves, by Sostrates, Mysis, or Pamphilus. The degrees vary with the actors' emotions, whether they are moved or not, or caught up in one passion or another.

Let us take matters even further: the epistolary style must be a simple one. It is said that you have to write a letter the way you speak (as long as you speak well, of course). Imagine a scale that runs from baker to king. There are so many social conditions differentiated by education, talent, birth, fortune, and there are so many simple styles that correspond to them. You must not use one where the other is appropriate. You cannot do so without offending taste and decorum. But the writer must also be true to himself, his personality, his age, his position, what he has been, what he has done, what he hopes, and what he fears. All these factors map out stylistic possibilities for him which he is able to implement if he has excellent taste. You cannot render all these possibilities in translation unless you have experienced them first and then you must master at your discretion the language you want to enrich with foreign loot. Strong languages break elegance when they try to transfer it. Weak languages dilute power. Try to imagine what a successful translation must be like!

The first requirement the translator has to meet is that he should master in depth the genius of the two languages he wants to deal with. He may have done so by means of some confused sentiment resulting from the habit with which you speak a language. But would it be useless to shed some light on the road of feeling and to give the translator a few hints to make sure he does not lose his way?

Sometimes you cannot find the words that correspond to the words you want to translate. This does by no means happen only to beginners or to those who do not know their languages well. When they are unable to find the simple words that are in existence they go looking for flaccid circumlocutions that cannot possibly take their place. We must tell them to study first and to learn their own language well. Once they have done so they will have problems only with syntactic constructions. They can then share those problems with people who have more experience because they have been using the language for a longer period of time. They will be able to solve those problems, at least in part, if they take to heart the concepts we are about to develop.

The first principle of translation is that you must use all stylistic features present in the original when both languages are amenable to this.

1 You must never tamper with the order of things, whether facts or arguments, since that order is the same in all languages and since it is tied to human nature, not the particular genius of different nations.

2 You must also preserve the order of ideas, or at least their parts. There must have been a reason, no matter how hard to detect, that made the author use one order rather than another. It may have been harmony, but sometimes it is also energy.

3 You must also preserve periods, no matter how long, because a period is nothing but a thought that consists of a number of other thoughts linked by an inner necessity, and those links are the life of those thoughts and they represent the speaker's main intention.

On the other hand, there are cases in which you can cut up periods that are too long. But then the parts you cut off are linked by an external logic and in an artificial manner. They are no longer parts of periods proper.

4 You must preserve all conjunctions. They are like joints that
   keep the parts together. Their position and their meaning
   should not be changed. They can be omitted only when the
   mind can easily supply them, that is when the mind propels
   itself from one part of a period to another and when the
   conjunction, if expressed, would merely hold it back and not
   help at all.

5 All adverbs must be placed next to the verb, in front of it or
   behind it according to the demands of harmony or energy.
   The Romans always gave them their place based on those two
   principles.

6 Symmetrical periods must be rendered symmetrically or in
   some equivalent manner. Their symmetry in the discourse lies
   in the relationship between a number of ideas or a number of
   expressions. The symmetry of expressions may be found in
   the sounds, the number of syllables, the length of the words or
   their endings, or the ways in which the parts of the period are
   arranged.

7 Brilliant thoughts should be rendered by approximately the
   same number of words to make sure their brilliance is preserved in the translation. Otherwise you will either brighten
   their splendor or darken it, and you are not allowed to do
   either.

8 You must preserve the figures of thought because they are the
   same in all minds. They can arrange themselves in the same
   order everywhere. This is the way to render interrogations,
   conjunctions, expectorations, etc. Figures of speech such as
   metaphors, repetitions, combinations of words and phrases
   can usually be replaced by equivalents in the other language.

9 Proverbs, which are popular maxims, and which can almost be
   considered one word, must be rendered by means of other
   proverbs. Since they only deal with things that are common in
   a society all nations have many proverbs in common, at least as
   far as the sense goes, even though they may be expressed in
   different ways.

10 All circumlocutions are evil: they are commentary, not translation. Yet necessity may serve as the translator's excuse if there
is no other way to make the sense known.

11 Finally, we must totally abandon the style of the text we
translate when meaning demands that we do so for the sake of
clarity, when feeling demands it for the sake of vividness, or
when harmony demands it for the sake of pleasure. This
becomes a second principle, which is the reverse of the first
one.

Ideas may present themselves under different guises and yet
remain the same and they may combine themselves or fall apart in
the words we use to express them. They may appear as verbs,
adjectives, adverbs, or nouns. The translator has four ways to
chose from. Let him take his scales, let him weigh expressions on
either side, let him bring them into equilibrium in various ways.
He will be forgiven all metaphors as long as he makes sure the
thought keeps the same body and the same life. He will do as the
traveler who gives a gold coin in exchange for various pieces of
silver, or vice versa, as he pleases.

These are a few very simple procedures. I venture to say they
will always achieve the desired effect. They will show the translator in need a way out of his predicament – the very way he has
been trying to discover for a long time if he has allowed himself to
be guided by instinct alone.

Gaspard de Tende, sieur de l'Estaing, 1618–1697. French
soldier and translator.

Extract from his *Règles de la traduction* ("Rules of
Translation"), published in 1665.

Moreover, I can say that this small book will be able to show how
one must avoid both of the radical extremes most translators seem
to succumb to. One is a certain liberty that degenerates into
license and that leads the translator away from the goal he has set
himself, namely to faithfully render all his author's thoughts. The
other is a submission that comes close to servitude and makes the
translator stick too closely to the words and phrases he translates,
without ever transcending himself. This goes to show that too
vulgar a stricture ruins all the grace and all the beauty of words
and that too high-minded a freedom changes all their sense. But it

is time to give a few more rules of translation, more precise in nature, for there certainly are sure and safe rules, in this art as in any other, that will produce excellent translators.

The first rule is to know both languages well, but Latin especially, to penetrate deeply into the thoughts of the author to be translated and not to make too lowly a submission to the words, for it is enough to render the sense with the most meticulous care and with utter fidelity, without leaving out any of the beauty or the images contained in the Latin.

The second rule is not just to render the author's sentiments as faithfully and exactly as possible, but also to try to render his own words in so far as they are necessary and important.

The third rule is to keep the spirit and the genius of the author you translate, while weighing whether his style is vague or pompous, whether it is the style of narration or of public speech. It would not be appropriate to translate a book written in a low and simple style into a book written in a sublime and elevated style. This is especially true of the Holy Scriptures or the *Imitation of Jesus Christ* since simplicity itself is beauty where certain ways of devotion are concerned. Similarly, it would not be advisable to translate orations that need to be treated with some latitude into a precise style, very cut and dry, nor should you translate parables, which need to be short and precise, into a style that would allow them more latitude. Indeed, a translator who wanted to render the simple style of the Holy Scriptures into a pompous style would produce a copy that would turn out to be very different from the Holy Original. Just as an excellent painter must endow a copy with all the features of the original he sets out to copy, and with its complete likeness, so must an excellent translator make the wit and genius of the author he is translating visible in his translation. And just as a well-made copy should not look like a copy, but like a real original, so should an excellent translation not look like a translation, but rather like a natural work, a perfectly pure production of the mind.

The fourth rule is to make people in the text speak and act according to their nature and their customs, and to express the author's words and his sense by means of terms in actual use that correspond to the nature of what you are translating. You should therefore not make a barbarian or a villager speak as if he were polite and civilized, because to do so would not correspond to the nature or custom of either. If you want to make a good translation you must not only make everybody speak according to his habits and inclinations; you must also see to it that the way he expresses himself is rendered in simple and natural terms that have already passed into current usage. Translators should not use manners of speech that have only just come into being because there are manners of speech that are not always good to write down, even if they may become so over the years.

The fifth rule is to try to match beauty with beauty and stylistic figure with stylistic figure when the same elegance is lacking in the two languages – which tends to happen rather often – and when you are unable to render the same beauty and the same stylistic figures.

The sixth rule is not to be longwinded, if only to make the translation more elegant and the sense more intelligible. There are translators who are unable to express matters with few words and in terms both appropriate and significant. They therefore resort to longwindedness and take liberties that little pupils in their first year at school would not be allowed to take. When they string out the words they translate – as they tend to do – they very often make the Latin lose all its power and sometimes they even change the author's words and his sense. That is why the shortest and most useful expressions are the best and most beautiful, since the ideal would be to translate line for line and to make the translation as short as the original.

The seventh rule is to always try to achieve the utmost clarity in discourse. For this reason excellent translators have admitted the necessity to cut up and restructure long periods, since a discourse that is put together in the first way and strung out in that manner is much less intelligible than a discourse that is shorter and more precise. We must therefore cut up Latin periods when they are too long, because our language is even more strung out and it would therefore keep the mind in suspense for too long, even if that mind always waits with great impatience for the end of what is being told.

The eighth rule is to run together periods that are too short when you translate an author whose style is clearcut and precise. Just as you sometimes have to cut up periods that are too long, so must you sometimes run together periods that are too short. It is best to keep an even temper in both cases and to use great discretion in trying to reach a reasonable solution in between two extremes.

The ninth and last rule is not only to look for the purity of words and phrases, as many people do, but also to try to make the translation even more beautiful by using felicitous expressions and stylistic figures that are often hidden and discovered only with great effort. It is just and reasonable not only to render the beauties of Latin into French, but also to take great pains to discover all those beauties wherever they may be hidden. If one Latin word, for example, finds itself in opposition to some other word in the same period, that opposition must be rendered by means of an opposition of two words in French as well. But since it is sometimes difficult to discover those felicitous expressions and those beautiful turns of phrase most beginning translators will limit themselves to the purity of words and phrases. They will not take too much trouble to keep the obvious beauty of the original, nor will they try to discover it where it is not immediately relevant.

These are certainly rules that will produce excellent translators. If you follow these rules you will be able to make use of a noble and high style in order to express a simple sense that would be too uninteresting and too low if it were rendered in all its simplicity. If you follow these rules you will learn to remain faithful to the sense of the words without distracting from their elegance, and you will be able to isolate their elegance without becoming unfaithful to their sense. If you follow these rules you will be able to produce a translation that is more beautiful, and so in a way to make the copy better than the original. Finally, if you follow these rules you will be able to enrich our language and to display its beauty so that even those who do not understand Latin may learn to speak and write better.

I would not be so attached to this little treatise if it were not as much the work of the most excellent translators and principal masters of our language as it is my own. I admit that my part has been limited to identifying the best ways of translating and the best figures of speech in their most excellent works. I can only hope that all those who read these rules will forgive the errors they find in them, since it is obviously impossible for a man who sketches the first outlines of any thing to do so with all the perfection time can bring to it. Such is the mercy I must expect from their generosity and the reward I ask of them for my attempt to alleviate the translator's burdens by proposing these rules of translation and by showing them how they will be able to embellish their translations.

Johann Jakob Bodmer, 1698–1783. German critic,
literary theorist, and translator.

Extract from his "Ninety-Fourth Letter" in *Der Maler der
Sitten* ("Painter of Morals"), published in 1746.

One generally hears talk about the spirit of languages and the
peculiar power of speech all nations are supposed to be able to use
in different ways to express their thoughts. Both are supposed to
represent the beauty of any given language, and a language is
called richer in as far as it is able to exhibit more specific instances
of this kind of beauty. We are at present living in a climate of
general zeal to polish and enrich the newer languages. It would
therefore be good for those who know languages to concern
themselves with giving to a language that lacks this or that
powerful locution or particular expression whatever characteristic beauty another language possesses. If languages were decked
out with these ornaments this unknown treasure would soon be
common to all nations and every language would, therefore, be
substantially enriched. It would also come close to achieving a
degree of perfection never hoped for.

I know of course that analogy, syntax, and similar elements do
not allow themselves to be transferred from one language into
another. However, these elements are to languages what the shell
is to the kernel because its value is never measured according to
the size, color, etc. of that shell. Their contribution to the real
treasure-house of language is therefore minimal. If one language
differed significantly from another only because it had its own
way of putting sentences together and using them in a particular
manner, those who know languages would find themselves badly
paid indeed with the profit they could derive from this. But there
are specific instances of beauty in each language that deserve all
our attention and they consist primarily of certain specific locutions that have been found suitable to express this thought or that.
The differences between nations themselves, the countries they
inhabit, their occupations, determine that these locutions should
differ from one language to another.

Man, who has nothing but images about him wherever he
looks, from childhood on, grows used to shaping an image of a
thing as soon as he thinks of it. He even goes so far as to make
himself an image of things he has never seen or heard described,
simply on the basis of the images he is already familiar with, and

he thereby claims to have some familiarity with the unknown. The difficulty we all encounter when we begin to study philosophy and to think in the abstract, without the support of substantial objects, shows sufficiently how deeply this inclination to think in images is ingrained in man's soul. Yet that thinking is very different according to the different occasions every man has for shaping his concepts. The peasant does not speak like the courtier, nor the soldier like the merchant. The peasant, whose house is designed for shelter only, whose food is destined to merely satisfy his hunger, whose furniture is limited to bare essentials, will produce little that is dainty or elegant in his speech. His locutions will be taken from simple things, from whatever is his everyday concern. The courtier, on the other hand, who spends all his days in splendid palaces, who sees nothing about him but art and treasures, whose food is prepared in the most special ways to whet his appetite and whose stomach, sick with looking on abundance, must be cured with foreign wines – will this lascivious and repulsive existence not fill his head in such a way that everything he says will be rich and soft and that all his thoughts are likely to appear in artificial images?

Whole nations are also subject to what can be observed in single individuals or classes: a rough, warlike nation and a weak, effeminate one will betray their different life-styles in their languages. Everyone admires the virile, generous nature characteristic of the English nation and expressed in its language. It is easy to see why it has taken so many figurative expressions from blood, death, and so on. The English fashion easy-to-use images of things other nations abhor. From childhood on they observe the casual way with which suicide is treated, the general contempt for life, the many fights among men and animals. For this reason an English writer of tragedies is under the obligation, so to speak, of putting the tragic ending of his story (or at least the effects of it) on the stage, before the spectator's eyes, whereas the shocked eyes and weak hearts of the French would never allow this. Where else might figurative expressions about ships and their construction and about navigation in general have come from, if not from those nations that are most concerned with those occupations and who spend their lives on ships? They are the ones who have shaped most of these concepts.

Even though different life-styles and different occupations cause people to express their thoughts in different ways, this does not prevent these expressions, dissimilar though they may sound, from being powerful and easy to use. They are that way, presumably, because they have grown out of an accurate knowledge of the image that has been their model. This becomes all the more obvious if we take a little time to notice that all figurative expressions, which make up the greater part of all languages, are nothing but similes. The better I know an image, the easier it will be for me to determine to what extent it is likely to give a clear shape and expression to my thoughts. The essence of a language is attained to the highest degree whenever an expression utterly exhausts the thought and when, moreover, the coloring and image a speaker uses to communicate what he is thinking to his neighbor are so powerful and so accurate that they convey the same ideas the speaker originally had of something and wanted to arouse in others. It is easy to see that the essential beauty of a language does not consist of empty sounds; rather it is rooted in the nature of things. The nature of things is the same in all countries, but both man's perception and his observation of it are different. Whoever fails to think of an appropriate word or even a decent image to express his thoughts may therefore be excused the first time, but if he happens to find the same thought powerfully expressed, be it literally or figuratively, in another language later on, and if he still refuses to speak in that way in the future he will render himself liable to the most severe punishment. Excuses to the effect that the expression is strange to him, or unheard of, should not be allowed to stand. Even if he has no concept of it he will at least stand to gain a small enrichment of his stock of words and images. If, on the other hand, he understands the expression, he will find that he has never yet fully grasped the thing in question, or at least not from the point of view from which he now finds it represented. He may therefore learn from it how endless representations and as many expressions may be shaped in speech on the basis of one well-known image. Whoever undertakes an intensive study of these peculiar expressions will soon find that the number of those for which we are completely without a concept is very limited and that most have come from those general concepts in which the nature of things instructs all men everywhere in the same way. Concepts such as fire, water, a king, are the same everywhere and everyone will soon understand in his own language what the flames of love are, the waters of sorrow, or the king of flowers. Even if the image is very strange the clear concept of the two words that have been combined cannot fail to determine the precise meaning of the whole. It is just that the qualities are adduced in a different way and that the manner in which they are represented, which is commonly called the power of speech, is not completely the same.

Those who love this true and inner ornament of language can find no better way to acquaint themselves with the general beauty of it and with particular instances than to take the trouble to translate into their mother tongue well-shaped passages of poetry and oratory that have been written in foreign languages. If they want to try to accurately preserve the author's thoughts with their particular power, they will soon find ample occasion to familiarize themselves with the riches and deficiencies of both languages. They will find many locutions in the foreign language they have no difficulty understanding, but they will stop short when they are required to translate these same locutions into their mother tongue. The way in which the words are connected may be very unusual; the power of the expression may strike them as strange; the thought may be represented by an absurd and disfigured image. In a word, they realize they have never heard this thought expressed in this way in their mother tongue. Yet they will often stumble on passages in which the locutions will seem watery and insipid to them when compared to those in which they usually see similar thoughts dressed. Yet it is easy to determine what needs to be done in that case. If the intention is simply to communicate the subject matter of the original in another language, the translator is under the obligation to translate everything as clearly and simply as possible, according to the spirit of his language. If an accurate translation is needed, however, which not only offers the thoughts contained in the original, but also retains all the ways and means the author uses to express his thoughts, this task must be undertaken with extreme precision and one should not be afraid of being accused of unheard idiosyncrasies or even downright mistakes.

Since translators have very different intentions, the world must of necessity be full of innumerable and wide-ranging translations. For some time now Germany has made it its special concern to familiarize its inhabitants with the writings of antiquity and many items of recent lore by means of translation. Most translators have been satisfied with merely communicating the subject matter contained in the original. I do not want to investigate with what felicitousness all this has been done. It is enough that everything has been said in pure and elegant German. Yet very few have gone so far as to try to make the German reader aware, in addition, of the manner in which the foreign author presented his subject matter to the German reader's eyes. The stern rule that has been enforced so harshly by certain overlords in the realm of the German language has marked all such attempts with public ridicule as with a painful iron, if it has not simply smothered them. A general, stupid-submission seemed to legitimize that tyranny.

Alexander Fraser Tytler, Lord Woodhouselee, 1747–1814. Scottish lawyer, judge, and academic.

Extracts from his *Essay on the Principles of Translation*, 1790.

I would therefore describe a good translation to be, *That in which the merit of the original work is completely transfused into another language, as to be as distinctly apprehended, and as strongly felt, by a native of the country to which that language belongs, as it is by those who speak the language of the original work.*

Now, supposing this description to be a just one, which I think it is, let us examine what are the laws of translation which may be deduced from it.

It will follow,

I. That the Translation should give a complete transcript of the ideas of the original work.

II. That the style and manner of writing should be of the same character with that of the original.

III. That the Translation should have all the ease of original composition.

In order that a translator may be enabled to give a complete transcript of the ideas of the original work, it is indispensably necessary that he should have a perfect knowledge of the language of the original, and a competent acquaintance with the subject of which it treats.

Where the sense of an author is doubtful, and where more than one meaning can be given to the same passage or expression, (which, by the way, is always a defect in composition), the translator is called upon to exercise his judgement, and to select that meaning which is most consonant to the train of thought in the whole passage, or to the author's usual mode of thinking, and of expressing himself. To imitate the obscurity or ambiguity of the original, is a fault.

If it is necessary that the translator should give a complete transcript of the ideas of the original work, it becomes a question, whether it is allowable in any case to add to the ideas of the original what may appear to give greater force or illustration; or to take from them what may seem to weaken them from redundancy. To give a general answer to this question, I would say, that this liberty may be used, but with the greatest caution. It must be further observed, that the superadded idea shall have the most necessary connection with the original thought, and actually increase its force. And, on the other hand, that whenever an idea is cut off by the translator, it must only be such as is an accessory, and not a principal in the clause or sentence. It must likewise be confessedly redundant, so that its retrenchment shall not impair or weaken the original thought.

Analogous to this liberty of adding to or retrenching from the ideas of the original, is the liberty which a translator may take of correcting what appears to him a careless or inaccurate expression of the original, where that inaccuracy seems materially to affect the sense.

I conceive it to be the duty of a poetical translator, never to suffer his original to fall. He must maintain with him a perpetual contest of genius; he must attend him in his highest flights, and soar, if he can, beyond him: and when he perceives, at any time, a diminution of his powers, when he sees a drooping wing, he must raise him on his own pinions.

It is always a fault when the translator adds to the sentiment of the original author, what does not strictly accord with his characteristic mode of thinking, or expressing himself.

Next in importance to a faithful transfusion of the sense and meaning of an author, is an assimilation of the style and manner of writing in the translation to that of the original. This requisite of a good translation, though but secondary in importance, is more difficult to be attained than the former; for the qualities requisite for justly discerning and happily imitating the various characters of style and manner, are much more rare than the ability of simply understanding an author's sense. A good translator must be able to discover at once the true character of his author's style. He must ascertain with precision to what class it belongs; whether to that of the grave, the elevated, the easy, the lively, the florid and ornamented, or the simple and unaffected; and these characteristic qualities he must have the capacity of rendering equally conspicuous in the translation as in the original. If a translator fails in this discernment, and wants this capacity, let him be ever so thoroughly master of the sense of his author, he will present him through a distorting medium, or exhibit him often in a garb that is unsuitable to his character.

But a translator may discern the general character of his author's style, and yet fail remarkably in the imitation of it. Unless he is possessed of the most correct taste, he will be in continual danger of presenting an exaggerated picture or a caricature of his original. The distinction between good and bad writing is often of so very slender a nature, and the shadowing of difference so extremely delicate, that a very nice perception alone can at all times define its limit. Thus, in the hands of some translators, who have the discernment to perceive the general character of their author's style, but want this correctness of taste, the grave style of the original becomes heavy and formal in the translation; the elevated swells into bombast, the lively froths up into the petulant, and the simple and *naif* degenerates into the childish and insipid.

From all the preceding observations respecting the imitation of style, we may derive this precept, that a Translator ought always to figure to himself, in what manner the original author would have expressed himself, if he had written in the language of the translation.

This precept leads to the examination, and probably to the decision, of a question which has admitted of some dispute, Whether a poem can be well translated into prose?

There are certain species of poetry, of which the chief merit consists in the sweetness and melody of the versification. Of these it is evident, that the very essence must perish in translating them into prose.

But a great deal of the beauty of every regular poem consists in the melody of its numbers. Sensible of this truth, many of the prose translators of poetry have attempted to give a sort of measure to their prose, which removes it from the nature of ordinary language. If this measure is uniform, and its return regular, the composition is no longer prose, but blank verse. If it is not uniform, and does not regularly return upon the ear, the composition will be more unharmonious, than if the measure had been entirely neglected. Of this, Mr. Macpherson's translation of the *Iliad* is a strong example.

But it is not only by the measure that poetry is distinguishable from prose. It is by the character of its thoughts and sentiments, and by the nature of that language in which they are clothed. A boldness of figures, a luxuriancy of imagery, a frequent use of metaphors, a quickness of transition, a liberty of digressing; all these are not only *allowable* in poetry, but to many species of it, *essential*. But they are quite unsuitable to the character of prose. When seen in a *prose translation*, they appear preposterous and out of place, because they are never found in an *original prose composition*.

The difficulty of translating poetry into prose, is different in its degree, according to the nature or species of the poem. Didactic poetry, of which the principal merit consists in the detail of a regular system, or in rational precepts which flow from each other in a connected train of thought, will evidently suffer least by being transfused into prose. But every didactic poet judiciously enriches his work with such ornaments as are not strictly attached to his subject. In a prose translation of such a poem, all that is strictly systematic or receptive may be transfused with propriety; all the rest, which belongs to embellishment, will be found impertinent and out of place.

But there are certain species of poetry, of the merits of which it will be found impossible to convey the smallest idea in a prose translation. Such is Lyric poetry, where a greater degree of irregularity of thought, and a more unrestrained exuberance of fancy, is allowable than in any other species of composition. To attempt, therefore, a translation of a lyric poem into prose, is the most absurd of all undertakings; for those very characters of the original which are essential to it, and which constitute its highest

beauties, if transferred to a prose translation, become unpardon-
able blemishes. The excursive range of the sentiments, and the
play of fancy, which we admire in the original, degenerate in the
translation into mere raving and impertinence.

We may certainly, from the foregoing observations, conclude,
that it is impossible to do complete justice to any species of poetical
composition in a prose translation; in other words, that none but a
poet can translate a poet.

It remains now that we consider the third general law of translation.

In order that the merit of the original work may be so completely transfused as to produce its full effect, it is necessary, not
only that the translation should contain a perfect transcript of the
sentiments of the original, and present likewise a resemblance of
its style and manner; but, that the translation should have all the
ease of original composition.

When we consider those restraints within which a translator
finds himself necessarily confined, with regard to the sentiments
and manner of his original, it will soon appear that this last
requisite includes the most difficult part of his task. To one who
walks in trammels, it is not easy to exhibit an air of grace and
freedom. It is difficult, even for a capital painter, to preserve in a
copy of a picture all the ease and spirit of the original; yet the
painter employs precisely the same colours, and has no other care
than faithfully to imitate the touch and manner of the picture that
is before him. If the original is easy and graceful, the copy will
have the same qualities, in proportion as the imitation is just and
perfect. The translator's task is very different: he uses not the
same colours with the original, but is required to give his picture
the same force and effect. He is not allowed to copy the touches of
the original, yet is required, by touches of his own, to produce a
perfect resemblance. The more he studies a scrupulous imitation,
the less his copy will reflect the ease and spirit of the original. How
then shall a translator accomplish this difficult union of ease with
fidelity? To use a bold expression, he must adopt the very soul of
his author, which must speak through his own organs.

If the order in which I have classed the three general laws of
translation is their just and natural arrangement, which I think

will hardly be denied, it will follow, that in all cases where a sacrifice is necessary to be made of one of those laws to another, a due regard ought to be paid to their rank and comparative importance. The different genius of the languages of the original and translation, will often make it necessary to depart from the manner of the original, in order to convey a faithful picture of the sense; but it would be highly preposterous to depart, in any case, from the sense, for the sake of imitating the manner. Equally improper would it be, to sacrifice either the sense or manner of the original, if these can be preserved consistently with purity of expression, to a fancied ease or superior gracefulness of composition.

It may perhaps appear paradoxical to assert, that it is less difficult to give a poetical translation all the ease of original composition, than to give the same degree of ease to a prose translation. Yet the truth of this assertion will be readily admitted, if assent is given to that observation, which I before endeavoured to illustrate, viz. that a superior degree of liberty is allowed to a poetical translator in amplifying, retrenching from, and embellishing his original, than to a prose translator. For without some portion of this liberty, there can be no ease of composition; and where the greatest liberty is allowable, there that ease will be most apparent, as it is less difficult to attain to it.

For the same reason, among the different species of poetical composition, the lyric is that which allows of the greatest liberty in translation, as a freedom both of thought and expression is agreeable to its character. Yet even in this, which is the freest of all species of translation, we must guard against licentiousness; and perhaps the more so, that we are apt to persuade ourselves that the less caution is necessary. The difficulty indeed is, where so much freedom is allowed, to define what is to be accounted licentiousness in poetical translation. While a translator endeavours to give to his work all the ease of original composition, the chief difficulty he has to encounter will be found in the translation of idioms, or those turns of expression which do not belong to universal grammar, but of which every language has its own, that are exclusively proper to it.

If a translator is bound, in general, to adhere with fidelity to the manners of the age and country to which his original belongs, there are some instances in which he will find it necessary to make a slight sacrifice to the manners of his modern readers. The ancients, in the expression of resentment or contempt, made use of many epithets and appellations which sound extremely shocking to our more polished ears, because we never hear them employed but by the meanest and most degraded of the populace. By similar reasoning we must conclude that those expressions conveyed no such mean or shocking ideas to the ancients, since we find them used by the most dignified and exalted characters.

I shall now touch upon several other characteristics of composition, which, in proportion as they are found in original works, serve greatly to enhance the difficulty of doing complete justice to them in translation.

1. The poets, in all languages, have a license peculiar to themselves, of employing a mode of expression very remote from the diction of prose, and still more from that of ordinary speech. Under this license, it is customary for them to use antiquated terms, to invent new ones, and to employ a glowing and rapturous phraseology.

2. There is nothing more difficult to imitate successfully in a translation than that species of composition which conveys just, simple, and natural thoughts in plain, unaffected, and perfectly appropriate terms; and which rejects all that constitutes what is properly termed *florid writing*. It is much easier to imitate in a translation that kind of composition (provided it be at all intelligible), which is brilliant and rhetorical, which employs frequent antitheses, allusions, similes, metaphors, than it is to give a perfect copy of just, apposite, and natural sentiments, which are clothed in pure and simple language: for the former characters are strong and prominent, and therefore easily caught; whereas the latter have no striking attractions, their merit eludes altogether the general observation, and is discernible only to the most correct and chastened taste.

3. The union of just and delicate sentiments with simplicity of expression, is more rarely found in poetical composition than in prose; because the enthusiasm of poetry prompts rather to

what is brilliant than what is just, and is always led to clothe its conceptions in that species of figurative language which is very opposite to simplicity. It is natural, therefore, to conclude, that in those few instances which are to be found of a chastened simplicity of thought and expression in poetry, the difficulty of transfusing the same character into a translation will be great, in proportion to the difficulty of attaining it in the original.

4. There is another species of composition, which, possessing the same union of natural sentiments with simplicity of expression, is essentially distinguished from the former by its always partaking, in a considerable degree, of comic humour.

5. No compositions will be found more difficult to be translated than those descriptions, in which a series of minute distinctions are marked by characteristic terms, each peculiarly appropriated to the thing to be designed, but many of them so nearly synonymous, or so approaching to each other, as to be clearly understood only by those who possess the most critical knowledge of the language of the original, and a very competent skill in the subject treated of.

6. There is no species of writing so difficult to be translated, as that where the character of the style is florid, and the expression consequently vague, and of indefinite meaning.

Wilhelm von Humboldt, 1767–1835. German philologist, educator, social thinker, and translator.

Extract from the preface to his translation of Aeschylus' *Agamemnon*, published in 1816.

This kind of work is untranslatable because of its peculiar nature, but untranslatable in a sense vastly different from that of statements usually made about the untranslatability of works of great originality. It has often been said, and confirmed by both experience and research, that no word in one language is completely equivalent to a word in another language, exception being made for those expressions designating purely physical objects. In that respect different languages are little more than collections of synonyms. Each language expresses a concept in a slightly different manner, with such and such a denotation, and each language places it on a rung that is higher or lower on the ladder of feeling. A collection of the synonyms of the main languages, or even only of Greek, Latin, and German (the kind of undertaking sure to earn widespread gratitude) has never been attempted, even though fragmentary attempts are to be found in the works of many writers. It would become one of the most attractive tasks if it were undertaken in the right spirit. A word is not a mere sign for a concept since a concept cannot come into being, let alone be recorded, without the help of a word. The indeterminate activity of the power of thinking condenses into a word just as light clouds originate in a blue sky. It has now acquired a being of its own with a certain shape and certain character, with a power to influence the emotions and the ability to procreate. If you were to think of the origin of a word in human terms that origin would be analogous to the origin of an ideal shape in the artist's imagination. To think of it in these terms is plainly impossible, merely because the act of pronouncing a word also presupposes the certainty of being understood and because language itself can only be thought of as a product of simultaneous interaction in which one is not able to help the other, but everybody at the same time has to carry in himself both his own work and that of all others. The artist's imagination, too, cannot be drawn from what is real; it originates in a pure energy of the mind and in nothing, in the purest sense of that word. Yet as soon as it has originated it enters life and is now real and lasting. What man has not created shapes of fantasy for himself – even outside the fields of artistic production or the production of genius – often in early childhood, and what man has not often lived more intimately among them than among the shapes of the real? How, therefore, could a word whose meaning is not immediately given through the senses be totally identical with a word in another language? It must of necessity exhibit differences and if one makes a precise comparison of the best, the most careful, the most faithful translations one is amazed at the difference that is there, where the translator merely tried to preserve equivalence and identity. It could even be argued that the more a translator strives for fidelity, the more deviant the translation becomes since in that case it also tries to imitate fine peculiarities: it avoids mere generalities and can, in any case, do little more than match each peculiar trait with a different one. Yet this should not deter us from translating. On the contrary, translation, and especially the translation of poets, is one of the most necessary tasks to be performed in a literature, partly because it introduces forms of art and human life that would otherwise have remained totally unknown to those who do not know a language, and above all because it increases the significance and the expressiveness of one's own language. For it is a marvelous feature of languages that they all first reach into the usual habits of life, after which they can be improved on *ad infinitum* into something nobler and more complex by the spirit of the nation that shapes them. It is not too bold an assertion to say that everything, the highest and the deepest, the strongest and the most tender, can be expressed in every language, even in the dialects of very primitive peoples we do not know well enough at this moment. This should not be taken to mean, however, that one language is better than another or that some languages are forever out of reach. It is just that in some cases the tones slumber as in an instrument that is not played, until the nation knows how to draw them forth. All signs of a language are symbols; they are not the things themselves, nor signs agreed on, but sounds which, together with the things and concepts they represent, find themselves through the operations of the mind in which they originated and keep originating in a real and, so to speak, mystical connection which the objects of reality contain as it were dissolved in ideas. These symbols can be changed, defined, separated, and united in a manner for which no limit can be imagined. A higher, deeper, or more tender sense may be imputed to these symbols, but this happens only if one thinks, expresses, receives, and represents them in a certain way. And so language is heightened into a nobler sense, extended into a medium that shapes in more complex ways, without any really noticeable change. As understanding of language increases understanding of a nation widens. What strides has the German language not made, to give but one example, since it began to imitate the meters of Greek, and what developments have not taken place in the nation, not just among the learned, but also among the masses, even down to women and children since the Greeks really did become the nation's reading matter in their true and unadulterated shape? Words fail to express how much the German nation owes Klopstock with his first successful treatment of antique meters, and how much more it owes Voss, who may be said to have introduced classical antiquity into the German language. A more powerful and beneficial influence on a national culture can hardly be imagined in an already highly sophisticated time, and that influence is his alone.

For he invented the established form – even if there is still room for improvement – which alone makes possible the rendering of the ancients into our language, now and for as long as German is spoken. He was able to do so only because of his talent and the dogged perseverance that enabled him to keep working indefatigably at the same object. Whoever creates a true form may rest assured that his labor will last, whereas even a product of the highest genius remains without consequence for further progress along the same path if it remains an isolated phenomenon lacking in such a form. If translation is to incorporate into the language and the spirit of a nation what it does not possess, or possesses in a different manner, the first requirement is simple fidelity. This fidelity must be aimed at the real nature of the original, not its incidentals, just as every good translation originates in simple and unpretentious love for the original and the research that love implies, and to which the translation must return. A necessary corollary to this conception is that a translation should have a certain foreign coloring to it, but the line beyond which this undeniably becomes a mistake is easy to draw. Translation has reached its highest goals as long as what is felt is not strangeness as such but merely a touch of the foreign. Where strangeness appears as such, probably even obscuring the foreign, the translator betrays that he is not up to the original. In such a case the unprejudiced reader's feelings do not easily miss the dividing line. If a translator goes beyond this, in fearful awe of the unwonted, and tries to avoid the strange itself, he destroys all translation and whatever advantages translation may bring to a language and a nation. Never mind that we have heard it said that the translator should write the way the author of the original would have written in the language of the translator, since such a thought must have been formulated without reflection on the fact that no writer would have written the same thing in the same way in another language, except for scientific matters and descriptions of physical objects. How else can it be explained that not the slightest shred of the spirit of antiquity has entered the French nation, indeed that not even the national understanding of antiquity (we cannot speak of single scholars here) has increased in the least, even though all the Greeks and Romans have been translated into French and some have even been translated very well in the French manner?

To come to my own work after these general observations, I have tried to approximate the simplicity and the fidelity described above. With every rewriting I have tried to remove more of what was not contained in the text in the same simple manner. The inability to reach the characteristic beauty of the original all too easily entices the translator to lend it a strange glitter from which, on the whole, a deviant coloring and a deviant tone will originate. I have tried to avoid obscurity and un-German turns of speech, but in the latter case no unjust demands should be made that might preclude higher advantages. A translation cannot and should not be a commentary. It should not contain obscurities originating in the vacillating use of language and in clumsy construction. Where the original only hints, without expressing clearly, where it allows itself metaphors whose meaning is hard to grasp, where it omits mediating ideas, the translator would go wrong if he were to introduce a clarity which disfigures the character of the text, and if he were to do so of his own accord. The obscurity you often find in the writings of the ancients, and especially in the *Agamemnon*, originates in the brevity and boldness with which thoughts, images, feelings, memories, suspicions are linked together as they originate in deeply-felt emotions, with no regard for mediating sentences to connect them. The more you enter into the poet's atmosphere, his time, the characters he puts on the stage, the more that obscurity vanishes and a greater clarity takes its place. You must allow the translation to proceed in a similar manner: you should not demand that what is noble, gigantic, and unusual in the original language should be easy and immediately intelligible in the translation. Yet ease and clarity always remain advantages a translator gains with the utmost difficulty and never through labor and rewriting: he owes it for the most part to happy inspiration, and I know only too well to what extent my own translation is deficient in this respect.

I have followed this edition [Gottfried Hermann's *Agamemnon*] as closely as possible since I have always hated the eclectic manner in which translators often choose arbitrarily among the hundreds of variants in manuscripts and critical emendations, trusting to a feeling which, of necessity, often leads them astray. The edition of an ancient author is the reconstitution of a document, if not in its true and original form, at least as close as possible to the earliest source accessible. It must therefore be the product of one mind, the result of historical precision and conscientiousness, of the whole treasure of scholarship that underscores it, and preferably of a consistency that permeates it from beginning to end. On no account should what is called the esthetic sense be allowed to interfere (even though translators in particular may believe they have a calling for it) if one does not want to impose ideas on the text which give way to other ideas sooner or later – the very worst fate that can befall those who adapt the ancients.

I have devoted the most meticulous care to the metrical part of my work, especially to the purity and exactness of meter, since that is the foundation of all other beauty, and I believe no translator could possibly exaggerate in this. Rhythm, as it rules among Greek poets, and especially among the dramatists, to whom no meter is strange, is a world of its own, so to speak, even when separated from thought and the music accompanied by melody. It represents the dark side of feeling and sentiment before it pours itself out in words, or when its sound has died away before it. The shape of all grace and nobility, the individuality of each character rests in it, evolves in free fullness, unites into ever new creations, is pure form, not weighed down by matter, and reveals itself in tones or, in other words, in what most deeply grips the soul because it is closest to the essence of inner conception. The Greeks are the only people we know who were in possession of such a rhythm, and it is this fact which, in my opinion, characterizes and defines them to the highest extent. What we find of it in other nations is imperfect: what we and even the Romans (exception made for a very few felicitous meters in their literature) possess is but an echo, both weak and uncouth. In judging languages and nations much too much attention has been paid to what I could call the dead elements, the outward diction: people always think everything is to be found on the spiritual level. This is not the place to go into detail, but it has always seemed to me that it is precisely the manner in which letters are united into syllables in a language, and syllables into words, and the way these words in turn relate to each other in rhythm and tone, which describes or determines the intellectual and, to no small extent, indeed the moral and political fate of nations. In this the Greeks were blessed with the happiest fate that can befall a nation that wishes to rule through word and spirit, not power and action. Among modern languages only German seems to possess the advantage of being able to imitate that rhythm, and whoever combines a feeling for the dignity of the language with a sense of that rhythm will attempt to endow the language with more and more of this advantage. For it can be increased: like an instrument, a language must be played to the hilt. The ear of many who have been misled by the arbitrary behavior of poets needs even more exercise, and the ear of those who do not read often must be especially trained in the less habitual meters. A translator, particularly of the ancient lyricists, can often win only by allowing himself certain liberties. Few will follow closely enough in the choric parts to examine whether he has used a syllable in the right way or not. Indeed, if two possibilities are equally right, many prefer a certain naturalness to the higher beauty of rhythm, as Voss so very aptly pointed out in his time. But here a translator must exercise self-discipline and abnegation, since only then shall he be cutting a path on which he may hope to have more fortunate successors. Translations are definitely works that should examine, define, and influence the state of a language at a given moment in time, as if measured against a timeless touchstone, and they must always be attempted again as if they were designed to last. Moreover, that part of the nation which is unable to read the ancients will learn to know them better through many translations than through one. Translations are as many images of the same spirit: each renders the spirit it has been able to grasp and represent, while the true spirit rests in the original text alone.

Friedrich Schleiermacher, 1768–1834. German philosopher and translator.

Extracts from "Über die verschiedenen Methoden des Übersetzens" ("On the Different Methods of Translating"), published in 1813.

We are faced everywhere with the fact that speech is translated from one language into another, and that this happens in many different ways. On the one hand this allows people who were originally as far apart as the length of the earth's diameter to establish contact, and texts produced in a language that has been dead for many centuries may be incorporated into another. On the other hand, however, we do not even have to go outside the domain of one language to encounter the same phenomenon. The dialects spoken by different tribes belonging to the same nation and the different stages of the same language or dialect in different centuries are different languages in the strict sense of the word, and they often require a complete translation. Even contemporaries who are not separated by dialects, but merely belong to different classes not often linked in social intercourse and far apart in education, can often understand each other only by means of similar mediation. Indeed, are we not often required to translate another's speech for ourselves, even if he is our equal in all respects, but possesses a different frame of mind or feeling? Sometimes we feel that the same words would have a totally different sense in our own mouth, or at least that they would carry more weight here and have a weaker impact there. We also feel that we would make use of totally different words and locutions, more attuned to our own nature, if we wanted to express what he meant. If we define this feeling more closely, and if it becomes a thought for us, we realize we are translating. Indeed, we sometimes have to translate our own words after a while when we want to make them really our own once again. This ability is not only exercised to transplant into foreign soil what a language has produced in the field of scholarship and the arts of speech and to enlarge the radius within which these products of the mind can operate. The same ability is exercised in the domain of trade between different nations and in the diplomatic commerce individual governments engage in: each is accustomed to talking to the other in its own language only if they want to make sure they are treated on a basis of strict equality without having to resort to a dead language.

We shall be able to distinguish two different fields [in translation] as well. They are not totally distinct, of course, since this is very rarely the case, but they are separated by boundaries that overlap and yet are clear enough to the observer who does not lose sight of the goal pursued in each field. The interpreter plies his trade in the field of commerce; the translator operates mainly in the fields of art and scholarship. Those who think of this definition as arbitrary, since interpreting is usually taken to mean what is spoken and translating what is written, will forgive me for using them, I am sure, since they are very conveniently tailored to fit the present need, the more so since the two definitions are by no means far removed from each other. Writing is appropriate to the fields of art and scholarship, because writing alone gives their works endurance, and to interpret scholarly or artistic products by word of mouth would be as useless as it seems impossible. For commerce, on the other hand, writing is but a mechanical tool.

Oral bargaining is the original form here and all written interpreting should really be considered the notation of oral
interpreting.

Two other fields are joined to this one, and very closely so as
regards their nature and spirit, but they are already transitional
because of the great multiplicity of objects belonging to them.
One makes a transition to the field of art, the other to that of
scholarship. If a transaction includes interpreting the development of that fact is perceived in two different languages. But the
translation of writings of a purely narrative or descriptive nature,
which also merely translates the development of a fact into
another language, as already described, can still include much of
the interpreter's trade. The less the author himself appears in the
original, the more he has merely acted as the perceiving organ of
an object, the more he has adhered to the order of space and time,
the more the translation depends upon simple interpreting. The
translator of newspaper articles and the common literature of
travel remains in close proximity to the interpreter and risks
becoming ridiculous when his work begins to make larger claims
and he wants to be recognized as an artist. Alternatively, the more
the author's particular way of seeing and shaping has been
dominant in the representation, the more he has followed some
freely chosen order, or an order defined by his impression, the
more his work is part of the higher field of art. The translator
must then bring other powers and abilities to bear on his work and
be familiar with his author and that author's language in another
way than the interpreter is. Every transaction that involves interpreting is concerned with drawing up a specific case according to
certain legal obligations. The translation is made only for parti-
cipants who are sufficiently familiar with these obligations, and
the way these obligations are expressed in the two languages is
well defined, either by law or by custom and mutual explanation.
But the situation is different in the case of transactions initiating
new legal obligations, even though on the formal level it may be
very similar to what we have just described. The less these can be
subsumed as particular cases covered by a general rule which is
sufficiently known, the more scholarly knowledge and circum-
spection are needed in formulating them and the more scholarly
knowledge of both language and fact the translator will need for
his trade. On this double scale the translator will, therefore, rise
higher and higher above the interpreter until he reaches his

proper field, namely those mental products of scholarship and art in which the free idiosyncratic powers of combination vested in the author and the spirit of the language that is the repository of a system of observations and shades of moods are everything. In this field the object no longer dominates in any way, but is dominated by thoughts and emotions. In this field, indeed, the object has become an object through speech only and in which it is present only in conjunction with speech.

What is the basis of this important distinction? Everyone perceives it even in borderline cases, but it strikes the eye most strongly at the outer poles. In the life of commerce one is for the most part faced with obvious objects, or at least with objects defined with the greatest possible precision. All transactions are arithmetical or mathematical in nature, so to speak, and number and measure help out everywhere. Moreover, an established usage of individual words will soon arise through law and custom even in the case of those objects which, as the ancients were wont to say, subsume what is more and what is less into themselves and are referred to by means of a gradation of words that sometimes carry more weight in common life and sometimes less, because their essence is not defined. It follows that if the speaker does not intentionally construct hidden indeterminacies or makes a mistake with intent to deceive or because he is not paying attention, he can be understood by everyone who knows both the language and the field, and at worst only insignificant differences will appear in linguistic usage. Even so there are rarely any doubts that cannot be immediately dispelled as to which expression in one language corresponds to an expression in another. Translating in this field is therefore almost a mechanical activity that can be performed by anyone with a fair to middling knowledge of both languages. It shows little distinction between better and worse as long as the translator manages to avoid obvious mistakes. But when the products of art and scholarship have to be translated from one language into another, two considerations surface that completely change the equation. If one word in one language corresponded exactly to a word in another, if it expressed the same concept to the same extent, if the declensions of both languages represented the same relationships, and if the ways in which they connect sentences matched, so that the languages would indeed be different to the ear only, then all translation would belong in the field of commerce, in so far as it would communicate only the contents of a spoken or written text. Every translation could then be said to put the foreign reader in the same relationship to the author and his work as the native reader, except for effects produced by sound and melody. But this is definitely not the case with all languages that are not so closely related that they can almost be considered different dialects. The farther languages are apart in time and genealogical descent, the less a word in one language will correspond completely to a word in another, or a declension in one language encompass exactly the same multiplicity of relationships as in another. Since this irrationality, if I may call it that, tends to pervade all elements of two languages, it is obviously also bound to make an impact on the domain of social intercourse. Yet it clearly exerts much less pressure there, and its influence is minimal. All words denoting objects and actions that may be of importance have been verified, so to speak, and even if empty, overcautious inventiveness might still wish to guard against a possible unequal value of words, the subject matter itself immediately restores the balance. Matters are completely different in the realms of art and scholarship, and wherever thought – which is one with the word, not the thing of which the word is only a sign, possibly arbitrary but nonetheless fixed – dominates to a greater extent. How endlessly difficult and complex the problem becomes here! It presupposes precise knowledge and mastery of both languages. How often the most expert and best versed in languages, starting from a shared conviction that an equivalent expression cannot be found, differ significantly when they want to show which expression is the closest approximation. This holds true both for the most vivid pictorial expressions in poetical works and for the most abstract terms denoting the innermost and most general components of highest scholarship.

The second consideration that changes true translation into an activity that is radically different from mere interpreting is the following: whenever the word is not completely bound by obvious objects or external facts it merely has to express, wherever the speaker is thinking more or less independently and therefore wants to express himself, he stands in a double relationship to language, and what he says will be understood correctly only in so far as that relationship is perceived correctly. On the one hand every man is in the power of the language he speaks and all thinking is a product thereof. He cannot think anything with great precision that would lie outside the limits of language. The shape of the concepts he uses, the nature and limits of the way in which they can be connected are prescribed for him by the language in which he is born and educated. Both his intellect and his imagination are bound by it. On the other hand every free thinking, mentally self-employed human being shapes his own language. In what other way would it have developed and grown from its first raw state to its most perfect elaboration in art and scholarship, except for precisely these influences? In this sense, then, the living power of the individual creates new forms by means of the plastic material of language. At first he does so only for the immediate purpose of communicating a passing consciousness, but gradually more or less of it stays behind in the language, is taken up by others and reaches out, a shaping power. Any verbal text is bound to die soon if it can be reproduced by a thousand organs in a form that remains the same always. Only those texts can and may endure longer that constitute a new element in the life of a language itself. As a result each free and higher speech needs to be understood twice, once on the basis of the spirit of the language that contains its component elements, as a living representation bound and defined by that spirit and conceived out of it in the speaker, and once on the basis of the speaker's emotions, as his own action, produced and explicable only in terms of his own being. Indeed, any speech of this kind can only be understood, in the higher sense of the term, when these two relationships have been perceived together and in their true relationship to each other, so that we know which of the two dominates the whole, or individual sections. We understand the spoken word as an act of the speaker only when we feel at the same time where and how the power of language has taken hold of him, where the lightning of thought has uncoiled, snake-like in its current, where and how the roving imagination has been held firm in its forms. We only understand the spoken word as a product of language and an expression of its spirit when we feel that only a Greek, to take one example, could think and speak that way, that only this particular language could operate in a human mind in this way and when we feel at the same time that only this man could think and speak in the Greek manner in this way, that only he could seize the language and shape it in this manner, that only his living possession of the riches of the language reveals itself in this way, as an alert sense of measure and euphony that belongs to him alone, a power of thinking and shaping that is specifically his own. This type of understanding is difficult to achieve, even in the same language, since it presupposes a profound and precise penetration into both the author's own nature and the spirit of his language. Imagine, then, what a high art understanding must be when it has to deal with the products of a distant and foreign language! Whoever has mastered this art of understanding through the most diligent cultivation of a language, the most precise knowledge of the whole historical life of a nation, and the living representation of single works and their authors, he and he alone may wish to unlock that same understanding of the masterpieces of art and scholarship for his own contemporaries and compatriots. But the risks increase when he prepares himself for his task, when he wishes to define his goals more accurately and surveys the means at his disposal. Should he decide to bring two people – two people who are so fully separated from each other as the author himself and the man who speaks his own language but not the author's – together into a relationship as immediate as that which exists between the author and his original reader? Or does he merely want to unlock for his readers the same understanding and the same pleasure he himself enjoys, with the traces of hardship it carries and the feeling of strangeness that remains mixed into it? How can he achieve the second goal with the means at his disposal, let alone the first? If his readers are to understand they must be able to perceive the spirit of the language that was the author's and to see his own peculiar way of thinking and feeling. Yet to help them achieve both those aims the translator has nothing more to offer than his own language, which at no point fully corresponds to the other, and his own person, he who understands his author sometimes more clearly and sometimes less so, just as he admires and approves of him to a sometimes greater and sometimes lesser extent. Is translation not a fool's errand if we think about it in this way? That is why people who have fallen prey to despair before they reached this goal or, if you prefer, before they reached the stage at which all of this could be clearly formulated in thought, discover two other methods for becoming acquainted with works in foreign languages, not primarily to gather their real artistic or linguistic sense, but rather to fill a need and contemplate spiritual art.

These methods forcibly remove some of the difficulties mentioned here while slyly circumventing others, but they completely abandon the concept of translation we are dealing with here.

These two methods are called paraphrase and imitation.

Paraphrase tries to overcome the irrationality of languages, but only in a mechanical way. It reasons as follows: even if I do not find a word in my language that corresponds to a word in the original language, I still want to try to penetrate its core by adding definitions, both restrictive and expansive. In this way it laboriously works itself through to an accumulation of empty particulars, caught between a troublesome too much and a painful too little. In doing so, paraphrase may possibly succeed in rendering the content with limited precision, but it totally abandons the impression made by the original, because the living speech has been killed irrevocably since everybody feels it cannot have originally proceeded from the feelings of a human being – and yet it has. The paraphrast treats the elements of the two languages as if they were mathematical signs that may be reduced to the same value by means of addition and subtraction. The spirit of the original language is not allowed to reveal itself where this method is used, and neither is the spirit of the language that is being transformed. Paraphrase often tries to mark the traces of the conjunction of thoughts in a psychological manner. It does so by means of interjected sentences it inserts like so many landmarks, even though the conjunctions themselves are unclear and attempt to obliterate themselves whenever it tries to do so. A paraphrase tends to usurp the place of commentary where difficult compositions are concerned and can, therefore, not be reduced to the concept of translation any longer. Imitation, on the other hand, submits to the irrationality of languages: it grants that it is impossible to render a copy of a verbal artifact into another language, let alone a copy that would correspond precisely to the original in all its parts. Given the difference between languages, with which so many other differences are connected, there is no other option but to produce an imitation, a whole composed of parts obviously different from the parts of the original. Yet, as far as the effect of the text is concerned, that whole would come as close as possible to the original as the difference in material allows. Such an imitation no longer claims to be the work itself, and in no way should the spirit of the original language be represented in it and be active in it. On the contrary, many things are bartered for the foreignness that spirit has produced. A work of this kind should merely be the same thing for its readers as the original was for its own readers, as much as possible and as far as the difference in language, morals, and education allows. The identity of the original is abandoned in favor of analogy of impression. The imitator does not try to bring the two parties concerned, the writer and the reader of the imitation, together in any way because he does not think a direct relationship between them is possible. He merely wants to produce an impression on the reader that is similar to the impression the original must have made on its contemporaries who read it in their own language. Paraphrase is more current in the domain of scholarship, imitation in that of art. Just as everyone confesses that a work of art loses its tone, its brilliance, its whole artistic essence in paraphrase, so too no one has, as yet, undertaken the foolish task of producing an imitation of a scholarly masterpiece that would treat its contents freely. Both methods, however, fail to satisfy the person who, permeated by the value of a foreign masterpiece, wishes to extend its operational radius to those who speak his language and keeps the stricter concept of translation in mind. Neither method will therefore be subjected to closer scrutiny here, since both deviate from this concept. They were discussed only because they mark the boundaries of the field that is our real concern.

What of the genuine translator, who wants to bring those two completely separated persons, his author and his reader, truly together, and who would like to bring the latter to as correct and complete an understanding of the original as possible without inviting him to leave the sphere of his mother tongue? What roads are open to him? In my opinion there are only two. Either the translator leaves the author in peace, as much as possible, and moves the reader toward him. Or he leaves the reader in peace, as much as possible, and moves the author toward him. The two roads are so completely separate that the translator must follow one or the other as assiduously as possible, and any mixture of the two would produce a highly undesirable result, so much so that the fear might arise that author and reader would not meet at all. The difference between the two methods must be immediately obvious, just as obvious as the relationship that exists between them. In the first place the translator, through his work, tries to replace for the reader the understanding of the original language that reader lacks. He tries to communicate to his readers the same image, the same impression his knowledge of the original language has allowed him to acquire of the work as it stands. In so doing he tries to move his readers toward his own point of view, which is essentially foreign to them. Yet if a translation wants to make its Roman author, say, speak the way he would have spoken to Germans if he had been a German, it does not merely move the author to where the translator stands, because the author does not speak German to the translator, but Latin. Rather it drags him directly into the world of the German readers and transforms him into their equal, and that is precisely the case under discussion. The first translation will be perfect in its kind when it can be said that if the author had learned German as well as the translator has learned Latin he would not have translated the work he originally wrote in Latin any differently than the translator has done. But the second translation, which does not show the author as he himself would have translated, but as he would have originally written in German if he had been a German, can have one measure of perfection only. It will be perfect if it could be certified that the original would have meant exactly the same thing as the translation now means to all German readers if those readers could be changed into experts who lived at the same time as the author. In other words, the translation will be perfect if it can be certified that the author has changed himself into a German. This opposition makes it immediately obvious that the procedure must be different in every detail and that everything would become unintelligible as well as unpalatable if the translator tried to switch methods in the course of one and the same project. I would merely like to add that there cannot be a third method with a precisely delimited goal over and above these two. The two parties who are separated must either meet at a certain point in the middle, and that will always be the translator, or else one must join up with the other completely. Only the first of these two possibilities belongs in the field of translation. The other one would be realized if, in our case, the German readers totally mastered Latin, or rather, if that language totally mastered them to the extent of actually transforming them. Much has been said about translations that follow the letter and translations that follow the sense, faithful translation and free translation and whatever other expressions may have become current. Yet these supposedly various methods must all be reduced to the two methods mentioned above, even though the faithful translation that follows the sense or the translation that is too free or too literal will not be the same according to one method as it is according to the other, if we want to talk about merits and mistakes. It is my intention, therefore, to put aside all problems related to this matter, which have been discussed by specialists, and to observe only the most general features of these two methods in order to reveal their particular advantages and disadvantages, the limits of their applicability and the ways in which they best reach the goal of translation. After such a general survey two things would remain to be done, and this essay can be no more than an introduction to them. Matters would be clarified even more if a set of rules could be designed for both methods, taking into consideration the different genres of speech. Furthermore, the best attempts produced according to either method could be judged and compared. But I must leave both of these tasks to others, or at least to another occasion.

The method which tries to give the reader, as a German, the impression he would get from reading the original work in the original language must, of course, first define what kind of understanding of the original language it wants to imitate. There is one kind it should not imitate and one kind it cannot. The first kind is a school-like type of understanding that laboriously bungles itself through separate parts, possessed by an attitude close to loathing, and therefore never acquiring a clear overview of the whole, nor a living comprehension of its connections. When the more educated part of a nation as a whole has no experience of a more intimate penetration of foreign languages, then let those who have progressed beyond this point be saved by their good genius from trying to produce this kind of translation. If they wanted to take their own understanding as a measure they themselves would be little understood and have little impact, but if their translation were to represent common understanding, their ungainly work could not be pushed off the stage fast enough. In such a time free imitations should first awaken and sharpen the desire for the foreign, and paraphrases prepare a more general understanding to open the way for future translations. But there is another kind of understanding no translator is able to imitate. Let us think of such wonderful people as nature produces every so often, as if to show that it is also capable of destroying the barriers of the common in isolated cases: people who feel such a peculiar kinship with foreign existence that they live and think completely in a foreign language and its products, and while they are totally preoccupied with a foreign world they let their own language and their own world become completely foreign. Or let us think of such people who are destined, as it were, to represent the power of language in its totality, and for whom all languages they are able to touch have the same value: in fact, they are in the habit of dressing up in them as if they had been born in them. These people have reached a point at which the value of translation becomes nil since their mother tongue does not even exert the slightest influence on their perception of foreign works. Since they do not become conscious of their understanding in their mother tongue but are immediately and totally at home in the foreign language itself, they do not feel any incommensurability between their own thinking and the language they read in. It is therefore obvious that no translation can achieve their understanding or ever portray it. Just as producing translations for them would be like pouring water into the sea, or into wine, so too they are wont to smile sympathetically from their Olympian height on all attempts made in this field, and rightly so, since we would not have to go through all this trouble if the audience translations are produced for was their equal. Translation therefore relates to a state of affairs between these two extremes and the translator must take it as his aim to give his reader the same image and the same delight that reading the work in the original language would give any reader educated in such a way that we can call him the lover and the expert, in the better sense of the word; the type of reader who is familiar with the foreign language, and yet that language always remains foreign to him. He no longer has to think through every single part in his mother tongue before he can grasp the whole, as schoolboys do, but he is still conscious of the difference between that language and his mother tongue, even where he enjoys the beauty of a foreign work in total peace. Granted, the definition of translation and its operational radius remain unsettled enough even after we have settled this point. We can only observe the following: since the desire to translate can originate only when a certain ability for intercourse with foreign languages is widespread among the educated part of the population, the art of translation will develop and its aim be set higher and higher the more knowledge and love of foreign products of the spirit spread and increase among those elements of the population who have exercised their ears and trained them without specializing in the knowledge of languages. Yet at the same time we cannot be blind to the fact that the more readers are predisposed toward this kind of translation, the larger the difficulties of the enterprise grow, all the more so if efforts are concentrated on the most characteristic products of a nation's art and scholarship – the most important objects for the translator. Since language is a historical fact there can be no right sense for it without a sense of history. Languages have not been invented and all mechanical and arbitrary work in and on them is stupid; they are gradually discovered and art and scholarship promote this discovery and bring it to fulfillment. Some of the ideas of a nation shape themselves in a particular way in one of those two forms in every excellent spirit and he will work in language and influence it to that end. His works must therefore also contain part of that language's history. This fact presents the translator of scholarly works with great, indeed often insurmountable difficulties, for whoever reads an excellent work of that kind in the original language, and is equipped with sufficient knowledge, will not easily overlook its influence on that language. He will notice which words and combinations still appear to him in the first splendor of novelty. He will observe how they insinuate themselves into the language through the special needs of the author's spirit and his expressive power, and this type of observation most essentially determines the impression he gets. It is therefore the task of the translation to transplant that very same impression in its reader. If the translation fails to do so the reader will lose part of what was intended for him, and often a very important part. But how can this be achieved? To start with particulars: how often will a word that is new in the original correspond best with one that is old and used in our language, so that the translator will have to replace it with a foreign content? If he did so he would have to move into the field of imitation if he wanted to reveal the language-shaping aspect of the work. How often, when he can render the new by means of the new, will the word closest in etymology and derivation not render the sense most faithfully, and yet the translator will have to awaken other connotations if he does not want to obscure the immediate connection. He will have to console himself with the thought that he can make good his omissions where the author did use old and well-known words and that he will therefore achieve in general what he is unable to achieve in every particular case. But consider the totality of the word-shaping work a master produces, his use of related words and roots of words in a whole array of inter-related writings. How does the translator propose to find a happy solution here since the system of concepts and their signs in his language is totally different from that of the original language, and since the roots of words do not correspond to each other in a parallel manner, but rather cut through each other in the most amazing directions? It is impossible for the translator's use of language to be as coherent as his author's. In this case he will have to be content with achieving in particular what he cannot achieve in general. He will reach the understanding with his readers that they will not think of the other writings as stringently as readers of the original would, but rather consider each one on its own, and that they should, in fact, praise him if he manages to salvage similarity with regard to the more important objects in particular writings, or even only in parts thereof, so that one single word does not acquire a number of totally different deputies or that a colorful variety does not reign in the translation where the original has strictly related expressions throughout. These difficulties reveal themselves for the most part in the field of scholarship. There are other difficulties of a more artistic nature to be tackled in the field of poetry and prose, and those are by no means smaller in size since the musical element of language that becomes apparent in rhythm and change of tone also carries a specific and higher meaning in this case. When this is not taken into account everybody feels that the finest spirit, the highest magic, or the most perfect products of art are lost, or even destroyed. Our translator will, therefore, also have to translate what a sensible reader of the original perceives as particular in this respect, as intentional, as influencing tone and mood of feeling, as decisive for the mimicking and musical accompaniment of speech. But how often (it is almost a miracle if one does not have to say always!) will rhythmical and melodic infidelity not be locked in irreconcilable combat with dialectic and grammatical fidelity? How difficult it is to avoid sacrificing something, now here, now there, as one swings to and fro, and to avoid what is often exactly the wrong result. How difficult it is even for the translator, when the occasion arises, to restore to his author with impartiality what he has had to take away from him before and not to succumb to a persistent one-sidedness, even unconsciously, because his inclination goes out to one artistic element above all others. If his taste in works of art gravitates more toward the ethical in subject matter and the way in which it is treated, he will be less inclined to notice where he has failed to do justice to the metrical and musical elements of the form. He will not ponder how to replace them; he will be satisfied with a translation that gets more and more diluted into the easy and semi-paraphrastic. If, on the other hand, the translator should happen to be a metrician or a musician he will put the logical elements last in order to grasp the musical elements completely. He will sink deeper and deeper into this one-sided enterprise and his work will become less and less felicitous. A comparison of the total effect of his translation with the original will reveal that he comes closer and closer to that schoolboyish inadequacy that loses the whole in the parts and does not even notice he is doing so. If he changes what is light and naturally expressed in one language into heavy and objectionable expressions in the other merely for love of the material similarity of rhythm and tone, a totally different overall impression will be the result.

Still other difficulties arise when the translator reflects on his relationship with the language he is writing in and on the relationship of his translation with his other works. If we except those miraculous masters for whom one cannot translate, as we said before, for whom many languages are as one, or for whom an acquired language is even more natural than their mother tongue, all others retain a sense of the strange, no matter how fluently they read a foreign language. How should the translator render this feeling of being faced with something foreign to readers to whom he offers a translation in their mother tongue? One might say that the answer to this riddle has been given long ago and that the problem has often been solved more than well enough in our case, since the more closely the translation follows the turns taken by the original, the more foreign it will seem to the reader. That may well be true and it is easy enough to ridicule this position in general. Yet if this joy is not to be bought too cheaply, if the most magisterial is not to be discarded in one and the same bathwater with the most schoolboyish, it will have to be admitted that an indispensable requirement of this method of translation is a feeling for language that is not only not colloquial but also causes us to suspect that it has not grown in total freedom but rather turned toward a foreign likeness. It must be admitted that to achieve this with good measure and in an artful manner, without disadvantage to one's language or oneself, is probably the biggest difficulty our translator has to overcome. The attempt seems to me to be the strangest form of humiliation a writer who is not a bad writer could impose on himself. Who would not like to allow his mother tongue to stand forth everywhere in the most universally appealing beauty each genre is able to give? Who would not rather sire children who are their parents' pure effigy and not bastards? Who would willingly force himself to appear in movements less light and elegant than those he is capable of, to appear stiff and brutal, at least at times, and to shock the reader as much as is necessary to keep him aware of what he is doing? Who would put up with being thought clumsy by trying to stay as close to the foreign language as his own language allows? Who would suffer being accused of bending his mother tongue to foreign and unnatural dislocations instead of skillfully exercising it in its own natural gymnastics – not unlike parents who abandon their children to acrobats? Finally, who would like to be exposed to the compassionate smiles of the greatest masters and experts who would be unable to understand his laborious and ill-considered German if they were unable to supplement it with their Latin and Greek? These are the sacrifices every translator is forced to make, these are the dangers he exposes himself to when he fails to observe the most delicate balance in his attempts to keep the tone of the language foreign. He will never escape from these dangers altogether, of course, because everyone strikes that balance a little differently. If, in addition to this, he also thinks of the inevitable influence exerted by habit, he may well fear that much that is raw and does not really belong will insinuate itself into his free and original production via translation, and that habit will somehow blunt in him the tender sense of his natural feeling for language. If he also ventures to think of both the great host of imitators and the slowness and mediocrity reigning among those of his readers who also write, he will be horrified at the volume of unlawfulness, genuine stiffness and clumsiness, and linguistic corruption of all kinds perpetrated by others. And yet he will probably have to answer for it since there is no doubt that only the best and the worst will not attempt to derive a false advantage from his endeavors. We have often heard this type of complaint, namely that such a translation must of necessity be harmful to the purity of a language and its peaceful development. Even if we want to put it aside with the consolation that there will also be advantages to counterbalance these disadvantages, and that true wisdom would counsel us to acquire as much as possible of the former while taking over as little as possible of the latter, since all good is mixed with evil, we shall nevertheless have to draw some consequences from this difficult task of representing what is foreign in one's own mother tongue. First, this method of translating cannot thrive equally well in all languages, but only in those which are not the captives of too strict a bond of classical expression outside of which all is reprehensible. Such bonded languages should look forward to a broadening of their sphere of influence when they are spoken by foreigners who need more than their mother tongue to express themselves. They will be perfectly suited to this. They may incorporate foreign works by means of imitations, or even translations of the other type, but they must abandon their first type of translation to languages that are freer, in which innovations and deviations are tolerated to a greater extent, to such an extent, in fact, that the accumulation thereof may well generate a certain characteristic mode of expression in certain circumstances. Another obvious consequence is that this type of translation has no value whatsoever if it is practiced only by chance in a given language, and in isolated instances. This would obviously fall short of its stated goal, namely to make a foreign spirit blow toward the reader. On the contrary, if the reader is to be given a notion, albeit a very weak one, of the original language and what the work owes to it, in partial compensation for his failure to understand that language, he must not only be given the totally vague impression that what he reads does not sound completely familiar. He must also be made to feel that it sounds like something different, yet definite, and that will be possible only if he is able to make comparisons on a massive scale. If he has read something he knows has been translated from other modern languages and something else that has been translated from the classical languages he will acquire an ear for distinguishing between what is old and what is not so old, provided the texts have been translated in the way described above. Yet he will have to read much more if he wants to be able to distinguish between works of Greek or Roman origin, say, on the one hand, and works of Italian and Spanish origin on the other. Even this is not the highest goal we try to achieve. On the contrary, the reader of the translation will become the equal of the better reader of the original only when he is able to first acquire an impression of the particular spirit of the author as well as that of the language of the work, and to develop a definite grasp of it by and by. He can do so only by exercising his powers of observation, but if he is to be able to really exercise them he will have to have many more objects of comparison available to him. These objects of comparison will not be available if only isolated works of masters in isolated genres are sporadically translated into his language. In this way translation will allow even the most educated readers to achieve only a very deficient knowledge of what is foreign, and it is inconceivable that they would be able to arrive at any judgment of either the original or the translation. This method of translation should therefore be applied extensively: whole literatures should be transplanted into a given language. The method makes sense only to a nation that has the definite inclination to appropriate what is foreign, and to such a nation only. Isolated works translated in this manner can be of value only as precursors of a more generally evolving desire and willingness to adopt this procedure. If they fail to inspire this willingness, the language and the spirit of the time will begin to work against them, and in that case they will be seen as mistaken attempts only and achieve little or no success. Yet even if this method of translation should prevail, we should not grow complacent and expect a work of this nature, no matter how excellent, to gather general approval. Since many factors have to be considered and many difficulties have to be resolved, it is inevitable that different opinions should develop as to which parts of the task should be considered of primary importance and which should not be considered in this manner. Different schools, so to speak, will therefore arise among the masters, and different parties among the audience that will follow these schools. Even though the method remains basically the same, different translators of the same work undertaken from different points of view will be able to exist side by side and we shall not really be able to say that one is, as a whole, more or less perfect than another. Certain parts of the work will be more successful in one version, others in another. They will not have fulfilled their task exhaustively until they are all taken together and related to each other and until it becomes clear how one translator attaches particular value to this particular approximation of the original, while another attaches particular value to another approximation, or how one translator exercises particular forbearance toward what is native. Until that happens each translation in itself will always be of relative and subjective value only.

These are the difficulties besetting this method and the imperfections essentially inherent in it. Once we have conceded these, however, we must acknowledge the attempt itself and we cannot deny its merit. It is based on two conditions: that a nation should know the importance of understanding foreign works and want to do so, and that its language should be allowed a certain flexibility. Where those conditions are fulfilled this type of translation becomes a natural phenomenon influencing the whole evolution of a culture and giving a certain pleasure as it is given a certain value.

But what of the opposite method that does not expect any labor or exertion on the reader's part since it aspires to bring the foreign author close to him, as if by magic, and to show the work as it would have been if the author himself had originally written it in the reader's language? This requirement has frequently been formulated as the one a true translator would have to fulfill and as being even higher and more perfect in nature when compared to the other one. Isolated attempts have been made, some of them even masterpieces maybe, which have clearly taken this as their goal. Let us now find out what they are like and see whether it would be desirable for this method, that has not been applied as frequently as the other until now, to be adopted, to be applied with greater frequency, and to supplant the other that is of dubious nature and unsatisfactory in many ways.

It is immediately obvious that this method does not threaten the translator's language in any way. Considering the relationship between his work and the foreign language, the first rule the translator must follow is not to allow himself anything that would not also be allowed in an original work of the same genre in his native language. Indeed, it is his duty first and foremost to observe at least the same care for the purity and perfection of language, to strive after the same light and natural style his author is famous for in the original language. If we want to make clear to our compatriots what an author meant to speakers of his language, we cannot think of a better formula than to make him speak in such a way as we imagine he would have spoken in ours, especially when the level of development at which he found his language is similar to the one our own language happens to have reached. We can imagine to some extent how Tacitus would have spoken if he had been a German or, more accurately, how a German would speak who meant the same to speakers of our language as Tacitus did to speakers of his, and good luck to he who is able to imagine this so vividly that he can actually make him speak. Whether this would happen if he let him say the same things the Roman Tacitus said in Latin is a question which cannot easily be answered in the affirmative. It is one thing to correctly grasp the influence a man has exerted on his language and to show it in some way, and quite another thing to seek to know how his thoughts and their expressions would have shaped themselves if he had been used to thinking and expressing himself in another language. The whole art of understanding all speech and hence also of all translation is based on belief in the internal and essential identity of thought and expression. Could a person who believes in this ever really want to sever a man from the language he was born into and think that a man, or even just his train of thought, could be one and the same in two languages? Or if they are different in a certain way could he then presume to dissolve speech to its very core, separate the part played by language from it, and let that core combine with the essence of another language and its power, almost as if by means of a new and almost chemical process?

But we have dealt with what is strange at too great length and it must seem as if we have been talking about writing in foreign languages rather than translating from them. The case, then, is simply this: if it proves to be impossible to write something in a foreign language that is worthy of and in need of translation as an art, or if this is a rare and miraculous exception at least, we cannot set up as a rule for translation that it should imagine how the writer himself would have written precisely what he has written in the translator's language since there are few examples of bilingual authors for the translator to follow. On the contrary, the transla- tor will have to rely almost totally on his own imagination for all works that do not resemble light entertainment or commercial transactions. Indeed, what objection could possibly arise if the translator were to tell the reader: here is the book just as the author would have written it if he had written in German, and if the reader were to reply: I am much obliged to you, just as I would have been if you had brought me a picture of the author just as he would have looked if his mother had conceived him by another father? If the writer's particular spirit is the mother of works of art and scholarship in a higher sense, his national language is the father. Artificial writings, on the other hand, lay claim to secret insights nobody possesses and can be enjoyed without inhibition only as a game.

That the applicability of this method is severely limited, indeed, that it is almost equal to zero in the field of translation, is borne out most obviously when one observes the insuperable difficulties it becomes entangled in where isolated fields of literature and art are concerned. We must admit that there are only very few words in colloquial usage in one language that correspond perfectly to words in another, so that one may be used in all cases in which the other is used and that one would produce exactly the same effect as the other in the same constellation. Imagine the incomparably greater extent to which this must hold true for all concepts, the more a philosophical essence is added to them, and it is therefore most true of genuine philosophy. In spite of differing contemporary and successive opinions, this is the very field in which language contains within itself a system of concepts that constitutes a whole whose isolated parts do not correspond to any in the system of other languages, precisely because they touch each other in the same language, because they connect with each other and complement each other. This observation holds true even for concepts like "God" and "Is," the primeval noun and the primeval verb. Even what is commonly believed to be general is illuminated by language and colored by it, even though it lies outside the boundaries of the particular. The wisdom of every individual must be dissolved in this system of language. Everyone partakes of what is there and everyone helps bring to light what is not yet there but has been prefigured. This is the only way in which the individual's wisdom is alive and able to really rule his existence which he completely summarizes in that language. Imagine that the translator of a philosophical writer does not want to take the decision to bend the language of the translation toward that of the original as far as possible in order to communicate an impression of the system of concepts developed in it, to the extent to which that is possible. Imagine that he would rather try to make his author speak as if he had originally fashioned his thoughts and his speech in another language. What choices are open to him in view of the dissimilarity between the elements of both languages? He must either paraphrase and fail to achieve his aim, since a paraphrase can never be made to look as if it had been originally produced in the same language, or he must transpose his author's entire knowledge and wisdom into the conceptual system of another language and therefore change all isolated parts, in which case it is hard to see how the wildest license might be kept within bounds. Indeed, it should be said that no one who has even the slightest respect for philosophical endeavors can allow himself to be drawn into so loose a game. I leave it to Plato to justify the transition I am now about to make, from the philosopher to the author of comedies. From the linguistic point of view this genre comes closest to the domain of colloquial conversation. The whole representation is alive in the morals of the people and the time and those, in turn, are perfectly mirrored in language, in the most lively manner. Lightness and naturalness in elegance are its prime virtue, which is precisely why the difficulties of translating according to the method just outlined are immense. Any approximation to a foreign language is bound to harm those virtues of diction. If the translation seeks to make a playwright speak as if he had originally written in its language, that translation will not be able to let him show too many things because they are not native to its people and therefore have no symbol in their language. In this case, consequently, the translator must either cut them out completely and destroy the power and the form of the whole in doing so, or else he must replace them. It is obvious that the formula will either lead to pure imitation if it is faithfully followed in this field, or else to an even more repulsive and confusing mixture of translation and imitation that cruelly bounces the reader back and forth like a ball between the foreign world and his own, between the author's wit and imagination and the translator's. The reader is not likely to derive any pure pleasure from this but in the end he is certain to be left with more than enough dizziness and frustration. If he follows the other method the translator is not required to subject himself to such self-willed changes because his reader must always remember that the author lived in a different world and wrote in a different language. He is bound only by the admittedly difficult art of supplying knowledge of this strange world in the shortest and most efficient way while allowing the greater lightness and naturalness of the original to shine through in all places. These two examples taken from the opposite extremes of art and scholarship clearly show how little the real aim of translation, the unadulterated enjoyment of foreign works within the limits of the possible, can be achieved by means of a method that insists on breathing the spirit of an alien language into the translated work. Moreover, every language also has its own rhythmic peculiarities, both in prose and poetry. As soon as the fiction that the author could also have written in the translator's language is established, the translator would be under the obligation to let the author appear in the rhythm of that language, which could disfigure his work even more and limit even further the knowledge of its particular character as provided by translation.

This fiction, which is the sole basis of the theory of translation now under discussion, goes far beyond the aim of that activity. Seen from the first point of view, translation is a matter of necessity for a nation in which only a small minority of people are able to acquire a sufficient knowledge of foreign languages while a greater minority would like to enjoy foreign works. If the latter became completely subsumed under the former all translation would be rendered useless and it would be very difficult to get anyone to take on this thankless labor. This is not the case when translation is seen from the second point of view. In this case translation has nothing to do with necessity. Rather it is a labor of recklessness and lasciviousness. Even if knowledge of foreign languages became as widespread as possible, and even if anyone who is competent had access to their noblest works, anyone who could promise to show us a work of Cicero's or Plato's in the way these authors would have written it directly in German at the present moment, would still be engaging in a miraculous endeavor that would be sure to attract more and more listeners who would be sure to become more and more intrigued. If, furthermore, somebody brought us to a point at which we would be doing this not just in our mother tongue, but also in another, foreign language, he would obviously be a master of the difficult and almost impossible art of dissolving the spirits of languages into each other. It soon becomes obvious, however, that this would not be translation, strictly speaking, and that its goal would not be the most precise enjoyment possible of the works themselves. Rather it would develop into more and more of an imitation and only those readers who were already immediately and independently familiar with those authors could truly enjoy such a work of art. The real aim of translation could only be to point out the similar relationships that exist in different languages between many expressions and combinations on the one hand, and certain inner features on the other. This would be translation's more limited aim; its general aim would be to illuminate a language with the particular spirit of a foreign master, as long as it is a master who is completely separated and cut off from his own language. Since the former is only an elegant and artificial game, and since the latter rests on a fiction that can almost definitely never be applied in practice, it is not difficult to understand why this type of translation is only sparingly practiced in a few attempts that serve to demonstrate that it cannot be more widely practiced. It is also not difficult to understand why only excellent masters who may presume the miraculous could work according to this method. Only those who have already done their duty by the world and therefore allow themselves to be drawn into an exciting and somewhat dangerous game are entitled to do so. On the other hand it is very easy to understand why the masters who feel they are unable to carry out such a task would look down with a certain compassion on the industrious efforts made by translators of the other type. They believe that they alone are engaged in that fine and beautiful art while all others appear to be much closer to the interpreter in so far as they, too, serve a need, albeit of a slightly nobler nature. Such interpreters seem to be all the more deserving of pity since they invest more labor and art than could possibly be justified in such a subordinate and thankless business. That is the reason why the masters will always advise the public to get by with paraphrases as much as possible, as interpreters do in difficult or dubious cases, and it is also the reason why this type of translation should not be produced at all.

Should we share their opinion and follow their advice? The ancients obviously translated little in that most real sense, and most moderns, deterred by the difficulties of true translation, also appear satisfied with imitation and paraphrase. Who would want to contend that nothing has ever been translated into French from either the classical or the Germanic languages? Yet even though we Germans are perfectly willing to listen to this advice we should not heed it. An inner necessity that is the clear expression of our nation's particular calling has compelled us to translate on a large scale. We cannot go back and therefore we must go on. Just as our soil itself has no doubt become richer and more fertile and our climate milder and more pleasant only after much transplantation of foreign flora, so too we sense that our language, which we exercise less than other nations do theirs, because of our Northern sluggishness, can thrive in all its freshness and completely develop its own power only by means of the most many-sided contacts with what is foreign. Coincidentally our nation, which respects what is foreign and is destined for mediation by its very nature, may be called upon to carry all the treasures of foreign art and foreign scholarship in its language, together with its own treasures in those fields and to unite them all into a great historical whole, so to speak, which would be preserved at the very center and heart of Europe. With the help of our language all nations would then be able to enjoy whatever beauty the most different times have brought forth, to the extent that foreigners can succeed in doing this in a pure and perfect manner. Indeed, this appears to be the real historical aim of translation as we have grown used to it now. If we want to attain this goal, however, we should practice only the first method discussed in this essay. Art must try to overcome as much as possible the difficulties besetting that method, which we have not tried to hide. We have made a good start but the larger part of the work still remains to be done. We shall have to go through many exercises and many attempts, in this field as in any other, before a few excellent works will come into being, and much is likely to shine at the outset that will later be supplanted by what is better. We already have many examples of the extent to which individual artists have overcome these difficulties, at least in part, or skirted them in a felicitous manner. Even if some who are working in the field are less able than we would like them to be, we should not be afraid that great harm will come to our language as the result of their endeavors. It must be established at the outset that translators work in a field that is theirs only, in a language in which translation is practiced to such an extent, and much of what should not be permitted to show itself elsewhere ought to be allowed to translators when they work in that field. Whoever tries to further transplant these innovations in an unauthorized manner will find only a few imitators, or none at all, and if we want to close the account after a reasonable period of time we can rely on the process of assimilation that is at work in all languages to discard again whatever has been accepted only because of a passing need and does not really correspond to its nature. On the other hand, we should not fail to acknowledge that much of what is beautiful and powerful in our language has in part either developed by way of translation or been drawn out of obscurity by translation. We are used to speaking too little and making too much conversation. It cannot be denied that our style had evolved too far in that direction over quite a long period of time and that translation has contributed more than a little to the reestablishing of a stricter style. We shall be less in need of translation for the development of our language when and if ever the time comes in which we are blessed with a public life that produces the kind of social behavior that is more meritorious and truer to our language, and gives more scope to the orator's talent. Let us hope that time will come before we have rounded the whole circle of difficulties in translation in a dignified manner.

Ulrich von Willamowitz-Moellendorff, 1848–1931. German philologist and translator.

Extracts from "Was ist Übersetzen?" ("What is Translation?"), the preface to his translation of Euripides' *Hippolytus*, published in 1925.

Only a philologist can translate a work of Greek literature. Well-intentioned amateurs try time and again, but if their knowledge of the language is defective the results they achieve are bound to be unsatisfactory. Yet translation does not belong to philology. It is above all the result of philological work, but a result neither planned nor foreseen. The philologist who dutifully strives to attain a complete understanding of a poem to the best of his ability is compelled against his will to express that understanding, and when he tries to say what the poet of antiquity said he tries to do so in his own language: he translates. Such has been my experience. Many of my colleagues share this experience, and not only where poets of original greatness are concerned, but also with regard to many texts we explain, as long as they exhibit a style that is fixed. We the philologists, dry as dust, who stick to the letter and analyze grammatical subtleties, also happen to be perverse enough to love the ideas we serve with all our heart. Servants we are indeed, but servants of immortal spirits to whom we lend our mortal mouths. Is it surprising, then, that our masters are stronger than we are? Of course the road that leads from such attempts to the completion of a translation worth its salt is a long one. Inspiration of the moment is not enough; it must be supplemented by long and thoughtful work of the mind if something useful is to be produced. That, then, is no longer philology; it is no longer our craft. We cannot do without our philology in this case, but it is not enough. Yet I do not think this should deter us.

Translations of Greek literature can come into being only if they are produced by us, philologists. To offer such translations to the German people is only one of the means we need to check the moral and spiritual decline our nation is moving toward at increasing speed. It is probably only a weak instrument, but only we philologists are able to give the gift of it, and we must do our duty as Germans. People do not want to know too much about us. That is their business, and for many of us the feeling is mutual. But they also do not want to know anything about the ideals we have devoted our lives to because we believe in them. That cannot leave us indifferent. Not because of our ideals: they are divine and they have proved that earthly power does not prevail against them, let alone the wild shouting of the modern mob of educators. But it is sad to observe how one's own country turns away from ideals, not just from the Greek ideal, but from any ideal at all. Gold, sensuality, honor, these are the gods they believe in; all the rest is words. The Greek ideal – or rather, the soul of Greece that has not died with the bodies of its people, nor will it ever – is perfectly capable of turning our people away from this, not just esthetically and intellectually, but morally too. That is why we need it. I do not know of much that could perform the same task as well. The real Goethe, and everything that implies, certainly can, and better for many people. But to understand him, not in the sense Goethe philologists understand him, but in such a way that we can accept his wisdom as a beacon for our thoughts and actions, we need the Greek ideal more than ever because it is presupposed by that wisdom. What represents the soul of Christianity is certainly also capable of performing that task and again, for many, in a better manner. But that soul can also co-exist with the Greek ideal since that ideal is one of the roots of Christianity itself. But as long as the churches give our children the stones of the catechism and the wood of devotional songs instead of the bread of the teachings of Christ, the result will all too often be the killing in man of the inborn striving after that ideal which tolerated every symbol, but not a single lie. Perhaps this situation will improve when scholars, both those who serve Christianity and those who observe the Greek ideal, will have understood that they belong together because both the objects and the method of their research are the same or, to put it more accurately, because they should serve the same master in the same manner. It will now be clearer what I mean when I say that the Greek ideal is indispensable to us and that it will remain so. If I believe that, how could I fail to recognize my duty to do what I can to open the way to that ideal? But how? Should I sing its praises, should I go sell it door to door, should I "popularize science" in the manner of natural scientists of the common variety? Far be it from me to do any such thing. Serious people in these equivalent fields of research obviously think and act the way everybody should who knows what scholarship is: a matter of work, a pursuit among men in which only those who take part in the work are able to participate. People must receive the ideal with their own hearts, they must believe in it and live accordingly, and to be able to do that they must see for themselves, they must make it their own. To hear something about the ideal, to satisfy a passing curiosity about it, to keep a few dead notes in one's memory: all that is of no use. Philology to the philologists, but the Greek ideal, its immortal part, should be available to everyone who wants to come, see, grasp. We must not give the audience a second infusion of our scholarly work to drink, we must not add to the sour hay of general knowledge in the cribs of its beloved magazines, we should not conspire with journalists to put people's thinking in chains by means of easy slogans and ready-made judgments, as they are wont to do. What we philologists should do, as I see it, is to make the ideal itself accessible to those who are looking for it, to put it before them and to show them how they should look at it, its importance, always. In so doing we give our nation the best we have, which is just good enough, and we give what only those possess who have really understood the Greek nation, its language, and its nature. That is what we have dedicated our lives to and it cannot be bought for less. But whoever has gathered such possessions should share them with everyone who wants to have them. *Noblesse oblige*. It is in this sense that I offer my translation to the public.

It is a translation, no more, but no less either. It is not free writing: we should not be allowed to do that, even if we could. But the poet's spirit should come over us and speak with our words. The new lines should have the same effect on their readers as the old ones had in their time on their nation, and as they still have now on those who have taken the trouble to do the necessary philological work. The requirements are that high. We know very well that we only meet them to a very small extent. But on this earth we can only do what is possible even though the impossible is required and we have to know the goal to find the way.

The audience thinks differently, of course: translation must be child's play since children do it, don't they? To lower the standards of education still further, translation from the Greek has superseded translation into Greek in our school examinations. Those who have seen samples of these achievements and are able to judge the success of the measure taken know that too much is required of students on paper, so that they can do too little with impunity. Many an experienced woman teacher and many an inexperienced girl who toil so hard in the honest struggle for bread that it would make a stone weep, are given a derisory sum by publishers who argue as follows: "Those are translations: everybody can do them." They are often "done" accordingly, of course, but the audience is satisfied with them. All you need is a grammar and a lexicon, and those who know the vocabulary or have been given a B in their exam on the language in question can manage even without a grammar.

And if we cannot render a particular expression (in fact we can almost never translate a single word because two words in two languages never cover each other completely where sense is concerned, with the exception of technical terms), we can still, even in German, express mild reproach that wounds more deeply for that very reason. We can express not just the thought of a speech, but its ethos as well. Here, too, it is important to spurn the letter and follow the spirit, to translate not words or sentences, but to take in thoughts and feelings and to express them. The dress must become new; what is in it must be kept. All good translation is travesty. To put it in more cutting terms: the soul remains but it changes bodies – true translation is metempsychosis.

There are excellent translations from Greek into German, so we are told. That is an untruth repeated with malice or without thinking. It is understandable for enemies of our culture to say so and to base what they say on the argument that there is no need to learn Greek. They achieve their aim that way: nothing is better capable of rendering the originals unattractive than translations are. But serious people ought to be ashamed to slap truth in the face like that.

Goethe cannot be absolved from the reproach that he is mainly responsible for the vainglory of German translation and its aberrations. Not through his practice, but through his theory. All he demanded of a translation was that it should help his linguistic knowledge along – and that knowledge was very deficient in all languages – to the extent that he would be able to understand the original in its own stylistic dimension. The more the translation was a hybrid and the more it seemed to hold on to the foreign style on the surface, the better it would perform that task – at least for him. He would be able to see the style of the original through the translator's lack of style, or at least he thought he would be able to. He wanted the foreign form mediated; he would mediate the foreign spirit himself. Moreover, Goethe was most inclined to acknowledge superior talent wherever he encountered it. He believed what Wilhelm von Humboldt and F. A. Wolf preached to him on the duties of the translator and he also believed in the translations made by his friends.

We do not have to go to great lengths, these days, to state that the metrical theories held by those great men are false, mere consequences of the fateful step Klopstock took with his hexameters. Our language and our literature owe very much to that step, but the attempt to equate quantitative poetry with accented poetry proved possible only because they simply did not understand the Greek language and the Greek meters. In truth language and meter belong together and it is monstrous to use the German language in conjunction with Greek meter.

It is very remarkable that the Romance languages are almost free from the aberrations of translating in foreign forms. That is because they possess an old culture, as well as established styles for their poetry. When Klopstock took the fateful step of wanting to become Virgil and Horace the Germans had neither a culture nor a well-shaped language, nor even a style, shaped or not. The task at hand was to create them and imitation was the means necessary to perform that task.

It has been done. A number of great men have created our language and our style. They themselves had their doubts as to whether the Germans deserved that gift. Nowadays they would deny it at once, I'm afraid. But deserved or not, the language and the style are there. To translate into German means to translate into the language of our great poets, and into their style.

This is how it is: whoever wants to translate a poem must understand it. Once that condition has been met he is faced with the task of recreating what is given in a certain language, with its attendant meter and style. Innovations can be made in the recreation only to the extent that the original offered something that was new to its language, in its time.

Bibliographical references

Texts belonging to both the Classical and Christian periods of Latin literature have been translated from the editions most readily available, which in most cases turned out to be the Loeb Classical Library volumes.

Shorter extracts of texts belonging to the French tradition, such as the remarks by Jean de Brèche de Tours, Voltaire, Prévost, Le Tourneur, Delille, Dolet, and Lemaistre translated here have been taken from Paul Horguelin's splendid *Anthologie de la manière de traduire*. Montreal: Linguatech, 1981.

Most of the texts belonging to the German tradition translated here have been taken from my *Translating Literature: The German Tradition*. Assen: Van Gorcum, 1977. Most of the translations have been revised to a greater or lesser extent. Only the longer texts will be found itemized in the list that follows.

Shorter passages from some English writings on translation included here have been taken from T. R. Steiner's *English Translation Theory 1650–1800*. Assen: Van Gorcum, 1975. Since they are well known and easily available they will not show up again in the list that follows. The short extract from Matthew Arnold's "On Translating Homer" has been taken from his *Essays Literary and Critical*. London & Toronto: Dent; New York: Dutton, 1924.

The following list represents an attempt to bring to the reader's attention important, less well known and less accessible texts on translating literature. As such it represents a somewhat "ghostly bibliography" of insights that are well worth reading, if only because they have preempted much of what is seen as new in current writing on the translation of literature. Since the texts themselves are identified within the body of this reader only the editions they have been taken from will be listed below.

Augustinus, Aurelius (Saint Augustine). *De doctrina christiana*. Turnhout: Brepols, 1982.
—— *Sancti Aurelii Augustini Opera Omnia*. Vol. II. Paris: J. P. Migne, 1841–1902.
Bacon, Roger. *The Opus Maius of Roger Bacon*. Ed. J. H. Bridges. London: Williams & Northgate, 1900.
Batteux, Charles. *Principes de littérature*. Paris, 1824.

Bodmer, Johann Jakob. *Der Maler der Sitten*. Hildesheim and New York: Olms, 1972.

Bruni, Leonardo. *Humanistisch-philosophische Schriften*. Ed. H. Baron. Leipzig: Teubner, 1928.

Carlyle, Thomas. *Critical and Miscellaneous Essays*. Vol. 1. New York: AMS Press, 1969.

Chapman, George. *The Iliads of Homer*. Ed. Richard Hopper. London: John Russell Smith, 1857.

Dacier, Anne. *L'Iliade d'Homère*. Paris: Rigaud, 1711.

d'Alembert, Jean le Rond. *Morceaux choisis de Tacite*. Paris: Desaint, 1784.

de la Motte, Antoine Houdar. *L'Iliade, poème. Avec un discours sur Homère*. Amsterdam: Depuis, 1714.

de Staël, Anne Louise. *Oeuvres*. Paris: Treuttel & Wurtz, 1821.

de Tende, Sieur de l'Estaing, Gaspard. *Règles de la traduction*. Paris, 1665.

Du Bellay, Joachim. *Défense et illustration de la langue française*. Paris: Didier, 1948.

Erasmus, Desiderius. *Opera Omnia*. Amsterdam: Gregg Press, n.d.

Fitzgerald, Edward. *The Variorum and Definitive Edition of the Poetical and Prose Writings*. New York: Doubleday, 1902.

Frere, John Hookham. *The Plays of Aristophanes*. London: Dent; New York: Dutton, 1911.

Holland, Philemon. *Pliny's Natural History. A Selection from Philemon Holland's Translation*. Ed. J. Newsome. Oxford: Clarendon Press, 1964.

Huetius, Petrus Danielus. *De Interpretatione Libri Duo*. The Hague: Apud Arnoldum Leers, 1683.

Hugo, Victor. *Oeuvres complètes de William Shakespeare*. Trad. François-Victor Hugo. Paris: Garnier, 1865.

More, Thomas. *The Complete Works of St. Thomas More*. Vol. VIII. Ed. Louis A. Schuster, Richard C. Marins, James P. Lusardi, and Richard J. Schoeck. New Haven and London: Yale University Press, 1973.

Pelletier du Mans, Jacques. *L'Art Poétique*. Paris: Belles Lettres, 1930.

Perrot d'Ablancourt, Nicolas. *Lucien. De la traduction*. Amsterdam: Mortier, 1709.

The Reader's Bible. New York: Oxford University Press, 1951.

Rossetti, Dante Gabriele. *Collected Works*. London: Ellis & Scrutton, 1890.

Schlegel, August Wilhelm. *Sämmtliche Werke*. Ed. E. Böcking. Leipzig, 1846.

Schleiermacher, Friedrich. *Sämmtliche Werke*. Berlin, 1838.

Shelley, Percy Bysshe. *The Works of Percy Bysshe Shelley in Verse and Prose*. Vol. VII. Ed. Harry Buxton Forman. London: Daley, 1800.

Tytler, Alexander Fraser, Lord Woodhouselee. *Essay on the Principles of Translation*. London: Dent; New York: Dutton, 1907.

Vives, Juan Luis. *Opera Omnia*. Valencia, 1782.

Voltaire. *Oeuvres Complètes*. Paris: Déterville, 1785.

von Humboldt, Wilhelm. *Gesammelte Schriften*. Berlin: Behr, 1909.

von Willamowitz-Moellendorff, Ulrich. "Die Kunst der Übersetzung." *Der Spiegel*. Berlin: Propyläenverlag, 1924.

—— *Reden und Vorträge*. Berlin: Weidmannsche Buchhandlung, 1925.

Index